algebra

the *x* and *y* of everyday math

algebra

the *x* and *y* of everyday math

michael willers

FALL RIVER PRESS

This 2009 edition published by Fall River Press,
by arrangement with Quid Publishing.

Fall River Press
122 Fifth Avenue
New York, NY 10011

ISBN: 978-1-4351-1400-5

Printed and bound in China

1 3 5 7 9 10 8 6 4 2

CONTENTS

ALGEBRA: AN INTRODUCTION

Mathematics means many things to many people. For some it represents all the beauty of the universe. Alfred North Whitehead (1861–1947), an English mathematician and philosopher, described pure mathematics as "the most original creation of the human spirit." For others, however, mathematics is a daunting subject, whether it takes the form of equations on a chalkboard or the fact that, however many times you try, the bills at the end of the month never add up.

These opposing perceptions are both too simplistic. On the one hand, even the most die-hard numberphobe can hardly fail to be struck by the beauty of something as simple yet compelling as the Fibonacci sequence when it occurs in nature; while, on the other, even the most avid mathmaniac would have to admit that many of mathematics' most beautiful ideas are shrouded in an air of impenetrable mystery, rendering them inaccessible to most of the population.

This air of otherness can be a most fearful thing. In fact, the fourth-century theologian St. Augustine of Hippo went as far to claim, "The danger already exists that the mathematicians have made a covenant with the Devil to darken the spirit and confine man in the bonds of Hell." A sentiment that many a bemused and disheartened student would doubtless agree with.

However, it doesn't have to be like this. Yes there are some difficult ideas, but there is also much beauty to behold. To study the nature of mathematics, one must consider what mathematics is really about, what makes it unique, and how it has developed.

This book aims to help you on that journey. Along the way, we'll meet many interesting and challenging ideas, but our aim is to connect them to the everyday world; and where that can't be done, simply to sit back and marvel at the beauty that the numbers unveil.

"The Laws of Nature are written in the language of mathematics."

Galileo Galilei (1564–1642)

WHAT IS MATHEMATICS?

Mathematics has been described in many ways. It has been called the science of number and magnitude, the science of patterns and relationships, and the language of science. Galileo, the famous Italian scientist who lived from 1564 to 1642, claimed that "The Laws of Nature are written in the language of mathematics." In fact, mathematics is all these things. It's a growing, creative, and dynamic field of inquiry. The explosion of mathematics is often hidden from the general population, but that has changed in recent years. Scientific discovery and debate—for example, that which surrounds global warming—have led to a desire to understand the underlying mathematical frameworks. The popular media have also played their role, and mathematics has been at the heart of such works as the Oscar-winning film *A Beautiful Mind* (an adaptation of the Pulitzer Prize-nominated book of the same name) and Dan Brown's bestseller *The Da Vinci Code*, to name but two examples. Even the fractal posters of a teenager's bedroom reveal an appreciation of mathematical beauty, whether or not people choose to see the numbers behind the patterns.

In spite of this, some people still see mathematics as a static discipline, isolated from the real world. This is chiefly the fault of an education system that spends most of its time reviewing material developed millennia ago. That's not to say that these topics aren't important and interesting, but it's rarely conveyed just how fluid a subject mathematics is, let alone how it has developed and grown over time. Mathematics has a rich history and within these pages we'll meet many of the fascinating mathematicians who shaped it.

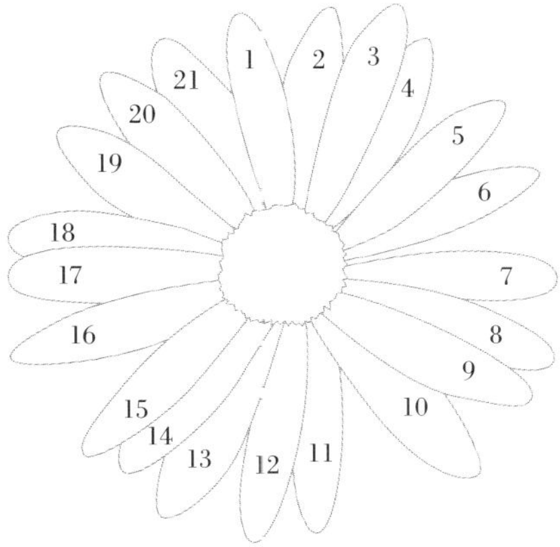

• The numbers of the Fibonacci sequence occur in many places in nature. In this case, there are twenty-one petals on the daisy.

What's more, mathematics continues to be shaped by remarkable individuals. Andrew Wiles, the English mathematician who famously solved "Fermat's Last Theorem" in 1994, and the popularity of Simon Singh's ensuing book, are both proof that mathematics is still growing and changing.

A Short History of Mathematics

As the discovery of a 30,000-year-old wolf-bone notched with tallies of five attests, the history of mathematics is ancient indeed.

The revelation that mathematics is not the exclusive domain of the human race—for example, it has been shown that crows can distinguish between sets of up to four elements—demonstrates that the rudiments of counting occur in other creatures. What's more, it begs the question: which came first, humans or mathematics?

Given mathematics' long and colorful history, it's hardly surprising that the contributions of great mathematicians go well beyond this field. Many of them were polymaths of one form or another, whether great scientists or profound philosophers.

A study of the history of mathematics is a study of the history of civilization. It can even be argued that the scientific revolution of the Renaissance came about because of the mathematical advances that allowed it. When Fibonacci (see pages 94–5 and 98–9) introduced Hindu–Arabic numerals to Europe in the thirteenth century, they allowed mathematics to be freed from the constraints of Roman numerals.

It must be pointed out that mathematics did not advance at the same speed everywhere. Its progress has ebbed and flowed. Ideas have been discovered and lost, and then refound. The flow of knowledge hasn't been all in one direction, and modern mathematics takes many different ideas from many different places. However, we have much to be grateful to Arabic and Persian mathematicians for. Situated between Greece and India they incorporated the best from both worlds, before their knowledge was exported back to Europe and the cradle of the Renaissance.

In the modern world, mathematics has become ubiquitous. Of course, it has always been around us in many forms. But today it plays a far larger role in the everyday lives of normal people than it ever has before. The degree of sophistication in a modern computer means that there's far more invested in technological wizardry, and with that comes some incredibly sophisticated mathematics.

But you don't have to be a computer whiz or a math genius to appreciate the beauty of numbers. The more you become aware of mathematics, the more you see its influence in the world around you—you don't necessarily have to understand every last equation. Even the most sophisticated strands of mathematics, for example chaos theory, can be found in such everyday images as the wisps of smoke from a cigarette or the swirl of cream in your coffee. As René Descartes said, "With me everything turns into mathematics."

"There is no royal road to geometry"

• Euclid is widely acclaimed as the "father of geometry," geometry being the basis of Greek mathematics.

The Nature of Mathematics

Mathematics is unique in that it can be both tangible and yet completely abstract at the same time. For example, at the simplest level, addition can be demonstrated with something as tangible as a handful of pebbles, but at the same time the sum $2 + 2 = 4$ is a generalized statement that can be related to any object, whether pebbles or pears, or it can even be a completely abstract expression that has no physical embodiment whatsoever.

$$2x(3x - 4) = 6x^2 - 8x$$

• The language of mathematics is quite beautiful, and transcends the boundaries of nations and continents.

Much of the history of mathematics has involved its development from a concrete discipline to a more abstract one. For the ancient Greeks, mathematics was a very practical subject, with geometry as its basis. A variable was represented as a length, the square of that variable as an area, and its cube as a volume. However, such a pragmatic approach caused the Greeks real headaches when it came to dealing with ideas that fell outside this paradigm, such as negative numbers.

Over the course of the intervening millennia, mathematics has become more abstract in form, and therefore more flexible. But this doesn't mean that its applications are any less practical. Even when an idea is pursued on a purely theoretical basis, it can eventually find its way into everyday usage. A good example is Joseph Fourier, a French mathematician (1768–1830), who worked with infinite series of trigonometric functions. During his lifetime, this subject was purely theoretical in nature, a mathematical puzzle to be solved, seemingly for its own sake. However, many years later the foundations he laid form the basis of analog–digital conversion. the technique that's used to turn analog sound waves into digital CDs.

The Language of Mathematics

One of the most fascinating things about mathematics is that it's a universal language. Though there are many different tongues on the planet, there's one common form of mathematics.

I have many exchange students in my classes, mostly from Europe and Asia. When they bring in their textbooks from their home country I can't understand a single word, but I do understand the mathematical symbols. As David Hilbert (1862–1943), a great German mathematician said, "Mathematics knows no races or geographic boundaries; for mathematics, the cultural world is one country."

Amazingly, mathematics may be universal in the truest sense of the word. And it is for this reason that the Search for Extraterrestrial Intelligence uses binary representations of π (see pages 18–19) and prime numbers (see page 16) to broadcast our presence to anyone who might be listening. The reason is that intelligent life on other planets would be unlikely to understand the word "hello" in any language. It's much more likely that they would have a concept of π, developed from working with circles; and, although their main mathematical system may well be different from our base-ten system, they're likely to understand the concept of binary (on/off or day/night).

• The five Platonic solids. These fascinating shapes have unique properties (see pages 52–3).

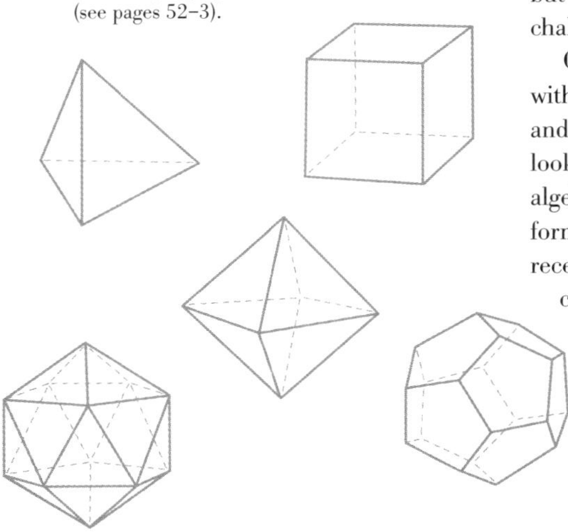

The nature of mathematics is such that the more you work with mathematics the more you appreciate it. The more you know about mathematics the more you are aware of it all around you. Mathematics is beautiful and dynamic. Its ever-present nature is its most powerful quality.

WHAT IS ALGEBRA?

The word algebra comes from a work by Al-Khwarizmi (see pages 86–7) called *Hisab Al-Jabr w'Al-Muqabala*, where "Al-Jabr" was to become "algebra." And Al-Khwarizmi is considered by some to be the "father of algebra."

When we're talking about algebra in these pages, we're really talking about elementary algebra. That's the algebra taught in high schools around the world. There are, however, other types—such as Boolean algebra (the algebra of logic)—that are somewhat accessible, but there are also many other more challenging forms.

Our focus is on the algebra that deals with arithmetic operations on numbers and variables; in other words, things that look like $3x + 5 = 9$. But, of course, algebra didn't spring into being fully formed: that sort of notation is relatively recent and stems from the seventeenth century and the work of René Descartes (see pages 116–17).

The first stage of development was rhetorical algebra. This took the form of full sentences, and dominated until the third century.

ON NOTATION

The notation used throughout is standard; but it's worth noting that to avoid confusion the use of *x* has been reserved for variables, while the symbol • is used to denote multiplication.

For the sake of clarity, numerals and words are used where most appropriate. Likewise, units of measurement are usually metric without conversions, because it is the numbers that are important.

Today, this style of algebra remains the bane of most students because it's all about word problems. Rather than solve $3x + 5 = 9$, we would have to solve something as archaic as, "a quantity increased itself three times then increased five more equates to the value nine."

Then came syncopated algebra, where symbols and shorthand were introduced. The work of Diophantus (see pages 64–71) is considered syncopated, as is the work of Brahmagupta (see pages 78–9). This was an improvement, but still required a lot of extra work compared to what came next.

The final stage in algebra's development, at least as far as we're concerned, was symbolic algebra. This is the kind we know and love today. When we write $3x + 5 = 9$, x is our unknown and we

> "Mathematics knows no races or geographic boundaries; for mathematics, the cultural world is one country."
>
> **David Hilbert (1862–1943)**

can solve it by using the other information available. The question is truly theoretical, and doesn't need to be tied to a practical example.

This notation came to its fruition with René Descartes, although it had been developed to a certain degree before him, Descartes' works are the earliest that a modern student could read without having real difficulty understanding the notation.

Alongside this, as we've already seen, algebra passed through several stages of increasing abstraction. During the Babylonian, Egyptian, and early Greek eras mathematics was geometric in nature, rendering the conception of zero and negative numbers absurd. Even when the algebra became syncopated, the aversion to negative numbers remained. As late as the fourteenth century in Europe negative numbers were still looked upon with suspicion.

Algebra then moved to a static equation-solving stage, and this is what you'll find within the rest of these pages.

So, without further delay, let's start our journey. Along the way we'll meet some fascinating characters and some equally interesting ideas, as well as a few problem-solving pages to get your mind ticking over. But let us start things off with some of the basics of algebra.

Chapter

1

Algebra Basics

In this first chapter we'll take a look at a few of the basics. We'll start off by meeting some of the different types of numbers, including the perfect, the radical, the irrational, and everybody's favorite number: π. Then we'll move onto some of the ways in which you can solve the more basic algebraic equations, as well as unveiling some of the fascinating history behind it all.

TYPES OF NUMBERS **Part I**

A number is just a number, right? Well, not really. Numbers are much like people: they belong to different groups. Just like a high school will have the cool kids, the geeks, and so on, so do numbers. In fact, some numbers are squares, some are perfect, and one is even golden. (The golden number—ratio really—is discussed in more detail on pages 100–1.) Before we meet the golden and perfect numbers, let's look at the most basic of classifications for numbers.

Number Sets

So, you're a cave dweller, and you're entertaining yourself by counting rocks. This represents the most basic of number systems, the "natural" or "counting" numbers: 1, 2, 3, 4, 5, and so on. This number set worked well for many years and still succeeds fabulously for many things. To expand upon this number set, however, requires a great leap in thinking. We will add a single number to the natural numbers, zero (see box opposite), to create a new number set: the "whole" numbers. The whole number set is 0, 1, 2, 3, 4, 5, and so on.

The next number set, which includes the whole numbers, is the bane of many of our lives. This is the set of "negative" numbers. Where would commerce and banking be without negative numbers? Positive and negative whole numbers are called integers. The integer set is …, −3, −2, −1, 0, 1, 2, 3, … and can also be expressed as 0, ±1, ±2, ±3, … and so on.

For the next set—the "rational" number set—you're out of your cave, agriculture has taken hold, and you're now raising chickens.

You wish to trade your chickens for a cow. So you meet with the cowherd and find out that the going rate for a cow is twenty chickens. You only have fifteen but you can use five of your brother Bob's to make up the difference. So, once you've butchered it, how much of the cow do you have to give Bob? Well, Bob gets $\frac{5}{20}$ of the cow, which simplifies to $\frac{1}{4}$ or a quarter.

These are fractions, or rational numbers. This set includes any number that can be expressed in the form $\frac{a}{b}$, where a and b are integers and b cannot equal zero—dividing by zero is a big no-no. Another way to express this is to say that rational numbers can be any "terminating" or "repeating" decimal. For example, $\frac{1}{4}$ is equal to 0.25, which is a "terminating" decimal. If, however, there was an exchange rate of nine chickens to a cow, and Bob had six chickens and you had three, Bob would get $\frac{6}{9}$ of a cow or $\frac{2}{3}$ or 0.66666..., which is a "repeating" decimal. Both of these types of decimal are rational.

So far the number sets we have met fit inside each other like Russian dolls, but the next stands apart from them. Numbers that cannot be expressed in the form of a fraction—in other words non-terminating and non-repeating decimals—are called "irrational" numbers. Two good examples of irrational numbers are π (pi) and $\sqrt{2}$ (the square root of two); these are weird numbers because they continue forever, without repeating or terminating.

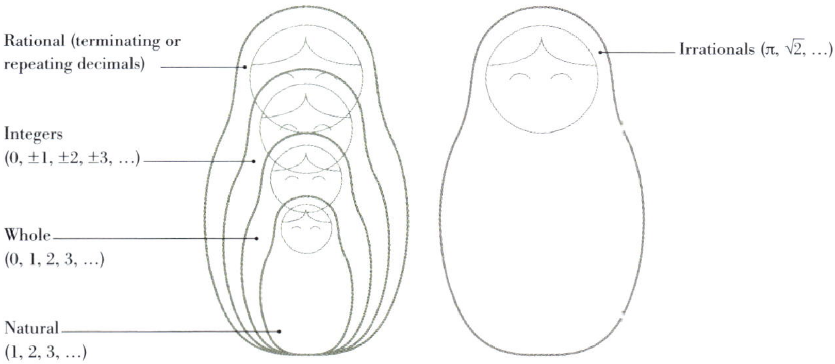

ZERO THE HERO

Although we use zero on a daily basis, few of us ponder its significance. Zero is a vital part of our place-value system. Without it 206 and 26 would look very similar indeed. Although this might seem obvious to us now, the theoretical leap required to develop a symbol that represents nothing is very impressive—and neither the ancient Greeks nor the Romans had a representation of zero.

The Indian mathematician Brahmagupta (see pages 78–9) was the author of the first text to treat zero as a number. It's sometimes said that you cannot ponder the infinite until you have pondered zero. In fact, this pondering of zero and the infinite is a big part of calculus—the nightmare of many university students. In essence, calculus is used in science, economics, and engineering to look at the infinitely large and infinitely small. So, not to put too fine a point on it, the appearance of zero was a huge moment in the history of mathematics.

TYPES OF NUMBERS **Part II**

Numbers have a varied social life, and they belong to different groups, like our chess clubs, gyms, or charities. On the previous pages we saw how numbers hang around in groups that fit within one another, like Russian dolls, and we also met the irrational numbers, which don't fit in; so here we'll look at a few other ways of grouping numbers.

Primes versus Composites

Prime numbers are a subset of the natural numbers. A prime is a natural number with exactly two distinct natural number divisors: one and itself. Or, to put it another way, a prime is a natural number that is evenly divisible only by one and itself. That is to say that if you divide a prime by any other natural number you will get a fraction or decimal. There are a couple of restrictions on primes: a negative number cannot be a prime; and one itself is not a prime.

Now, composite numbers represent the "opposite" of primes. A composite number is a natural number that has a positive divisor other than one and itself. This means that composite numbers represent all the natural numbers that are not prime numbers, except one. The number one is neither a prime number nor a composite number. There's always an odd one out.

Square Numbers

When we read $4^2 = 16$, we say "four squared equals sixteen." Ever wonder why we call it "squared"? Well, the Greeks were big on geometry and applied it to numbers as well. Sixteen is a square number because you can arrange sixteen dots to form a four-by-four square. In fact, sixteen is the fourth square number, or $n = 4$. Most of us are familiar with the square number set 1, 4, 9, 16, 25, and so on—it's the diagonal on your old school multiplication grid—and the formula for finding a square number is n^2.

Triangular Numbers

A less well-known set is that of the triangular numbers: 1, 3, 6, 10, 15, 21, and so on. As with the square numbers, the triangular numbers get their name because they can be formed into triangles of dots.

It's interesting to note that there are some numbers that are both square and triangular. In fact, we've already met the first: it's the number one. After that we move onto thirty-six before we meet

• The first few square numbers (1, 4, 9, 16) arranged as dots.

THE GEOMETRY OF NUMBERS

Like square and triangular numbers there are many geometric (or figurate) number sets, and the table below shows the first few along with the formulas that you can use to find them—just replace *n* with any number and you'll find the corresponding geometric number. Geometric numbers even exist in three dimensions; for example, there are "tetrahedral" numbers that are the sums of triangular numbers and form a pyramid with a triangular base.

Number Type	First Few Numbers	Formula
Triangular	1, 3, 6, 10, 15, …	$\frac{(n)(n+1)}{2}$
Square	1, 4, 9, 16, 25, …	n^2
Pentagonal	1, 5, 12, 22, 35, …	$\frac{(n)\ 3n-1)}{2}$
Hexagonal	1, 6, 15, 28, 45, …	$(n)(2n-1)$
Heptagonal	1, 7, 18, 34, 55, …	$\frac{(n)(5n-3)}{2}$

another number that can be drawn in dot form both as a triangle and a square, after that it's 1225, then 41616—the gaps become bigger as the numbers get higher. But geometric numbers don't stop there, more are discussed above.

• Thirty-six expressed as dots, showing that it is both a square number and a triangular number.

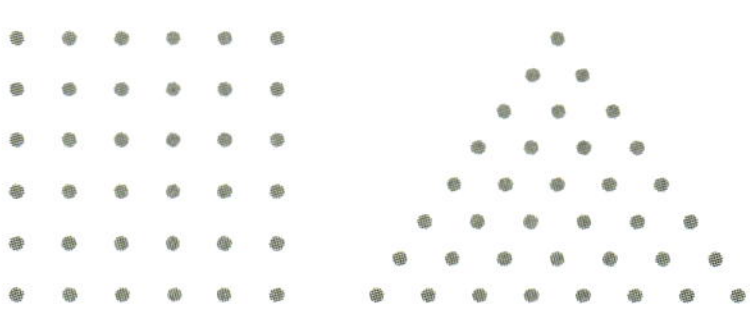

Perfect Numbers

A "perfect" number is one for which the sum of all its proper divisors (whole-number divisors) is equal to the number. This is best shown with an example: six is a perfect number because the proper divisors of six are one, two, and three. These numbers also total six. Perfect numbers are quite rare and really neat. The next perfect number is twenty-eight. The divisors of twenty-eight are one, two, four, seven, and fourteen. If we add these together then we get twenty-eight.

We don't see another perfect number until 496, and after that it's 8128.

A SHORT HISTORY OF PI

Pi (π) is like a rock star. One Christmas my wife gave me a shirt with π on it. Whenever I wear it, strangers come up and say: "Cool shirt!" People like π. They like the idea of π; it connects them to mathematics beyond the mundane arithmetic of everyday life. For many, it's their first introduction to infinity. So here's a short history of π, its use, and significance.

What Is Pi?

Pi, or π, is defined as the ratio of the circumference of a circle to its diameter:

$$\pi = \frac{circumference}{diameter} = \frac{c}{d}$$

This often leads to confusion among people because they are also told that π is "irrational" (see page 15) which means that it cannot be expressed as a fraction. The thing we need to remember is that a fraction is $\frac{a}{b}$ where a and b are integers. But with π either the circumference or the diameter will be irrational. This is interesting and strange: it means that if you can write the value of the diameter, you will never be able to write the exact value of the circumference as a decimal, and vice versa.

The idea of π as a constant has been around for millennia. The Egyptians

PI THROUGH THE AGES

Source	Year	Estimate
Rhind papyrus	c. 1650 BCE	3.16045
Archimedes (average of the bounds)	250 BCE	3.1418
Ptolemy	150 CE	3.14166
Brahmagupta	640 CE	3.1622 ($\sqrt{10}$)
Al-Khwarizmi	800 CE	3.1416
Fibonacci	1220 CE	3.141818

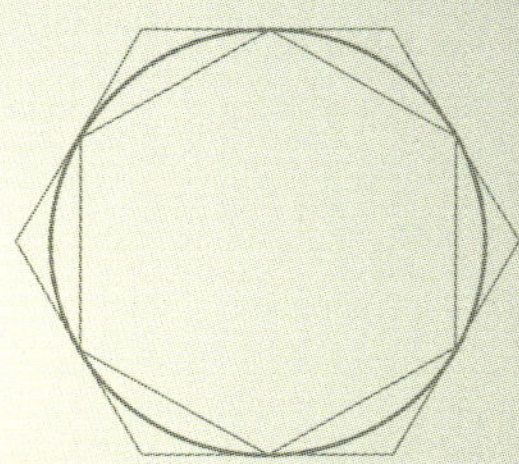

• Archimedes' method for estimating π involved drawing regular polyhedra inside and outside a circle, measuring them, and averaging their "bounds."

estimated it at $\frac{25}{8}$ (or 3.125) while the Mesopotamians gave it a value of $\sqrt{10}$ (or 3.162).

Archimedes was the first to examine π in depth. By using polygons both inside and outside the circle, and calculating their perimeters, he was able to estimate for π between $\frac{223}{71}$ and $\frac{22}{7}$, which is where the common appoximation of π as $\frac{22}{7}$ comes from. Since Archimedes' time the accuracy of π has been increasing, though some early estimates were better than those that followed (see table). Now, thanks largely to the advent of computers, we know π to billions of digits.

JOHN WALLIS

The third of five children, John Wallis, whose series we've seen below, was born in Ashford, England in 1616. In 1631 his brother introduced him to arithmetic, then in 1632 he entered Emmanuel College, Cambridge, receiving a BA and Masters by 1640. During the English Civil War (1642–51), Wallis used his mathematical skills to decode Royalist messages for the Parliamentarians—cryptography is something we'll get on to in the last chapter.

In 1649, Wallis was appointed to the Savilian Chair of Geometry at Oxford University, a post he held until his death in 1703. Wallis helped with the development of calculus and is known for being the first to use the symbol ∞ for infinity.

Formulas for Pi

The symbol π (its modern mathematical meaning) was introduced by William Jones in 1706 in his book *Synopsis Palmariorum Mathesios*. However, π can also be represented as an infinite series of numbers. The fourteenth-century Indian mathematician and astronomer, Madhava, produced the series:

$$\frac{\pi}{4} = 1 - \frac{1}{3} + \frac{1}{5} - \frac{1}{7} + \frac{1}{9} \ldots$$

This can be used to estimate π, but it's slow. The eighteenth-century Swiss mathematician Leonhard Euler (see pages 140–1) used the series:

$$\frac{\pi^2}{6} = 1 + \frac{1}{2^2} + \frac{1}{3^2} + \frac{1}{4^2} \ldots$$

While another interesting series was given by John Wallis (see box above), which he published in 1656. It starts off with:

$$\frac{\pi}{2} = \frac{2}{1} \cdot \frac{2}{3} \cdot \frac{4}{3} \cdot \frac{4}{5} \cdot \frac{6}{5} \ldots$$

Without delving too deeply into the mathematics, these series show some of the many neat properties of π; and perhaps this is the reason for its enduring appeal. What's more, from the speedometer and odometer in your car to the calculation of the volume of every tin can, π's impact on everyday life can be felt everywhere.

ORDER OF OPERATIONS

Imagine living in a place where people ignored the rules of the road—I could describe the nightmare of being stuck at a four-way stop in my hometown, but there aren't enough pages in this book. The point is, that without rules some people would drive on the right, some on the left, some would stop at red lights, some at green—it would be anarchy.

The same is true for mathematics. So, before we get stuck into some equations we need to set the ground rules. Without rules different people would get different answers to the same question. For example, let's look at how Sid and Nancy solve the problem: $3 + 4 \cdot 5$.

Sid is a straight-ahead sort, so he adds three to four giving seven, then multiplies that by five to give thirty-five. Nancy, on the other hand, does things differently: four times five is twenty, which added to three gives twenty-three. They get different answers and a fight ensues.

So who's right? Well, it's Nancy. And here's why.

In mathematics there is a certain order in which mathematical operations must be done. There's a mnemonic to help: BEDMAS (sometimes BODMAS or PEDMAS). This translates as:

Brackets (or **P**arentheses)

Exponents (or **O**rders)

Division and **M**ultiplication

Addition and **S**ubtraction

You start with things inside brackets (parentheses) then move onto exponents (orders). Multiplication and division are all done at the same time, starting from the left and moving to the right. Then comes addition and subtraction—again, these are done at the same time, starting from the left and moving to the right. Higher functions, such as logarithms and trigonometric functions, happen at the exponent level.

The levels make sense if you think about the operations that are performed. Addition is the most basic operation—the first we learn. Multiplication is really just successive additions; that is to say, "two times five" is really two added to itself five times:

$$2 \cdot 5 = 2 + 2 + 2 + 2 + 2$$

Next, an exponent just represents successive multiplications, for example:

$$2^5 = 2 \cdot 2 \cdot 2 \cdot 2 \cdot 2$$

So, as you can see, each operation builds on the previous one as we move through the order of operations.

Nested Brackets

Nested brackets (a set of brackets inside another set) sometimes cause problems when trying to follow BEDMAS. So let's look at an example:

$$9 + 3(8 - 2(6 - 5))$$

To simplify this we evaluate from the inside out. Therefore, we first subtract $(6 - 5)$ to get 1. Now the expression is:

$$9 + 3(8 - 2(1))$$

And $2(1)$ is really just 2 which gives:

$$9 + 3(8 - 2)$$

Next we evaluate our final bracket, to get 6 and the expression is:

$$9 + 3(6)$$

This becomes $9 + 18$ which equals 27.

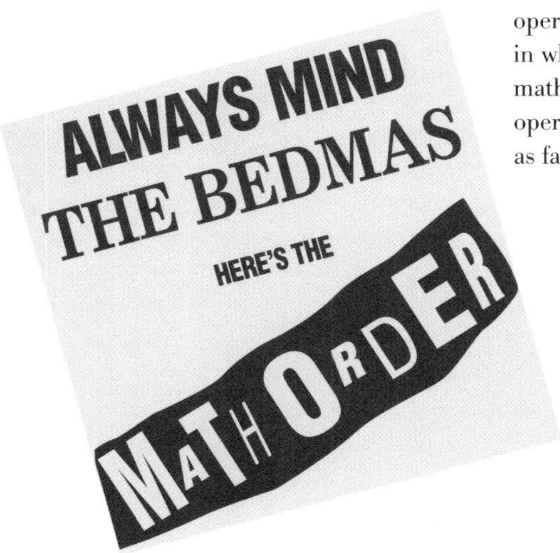

Grouping

Another problem people confront is grouping, which is often implied and can cause confusion. As an example $x \cdot x - 3$ is not the same as $x \cdot (x - 3)$. The former is really $x^2 - 3$ while the latter is $x^2 - 3x$. So when someone writes ½x do they mean "one half times x" or do they mean "one divided by two xs"? If x had a value of 10 the first result would be 5 while the second would be 0.05—a big difference. This is where grouping helps; if you want to say "half times x" you could write $(\frac{1}{2})x$ to avoid confusion. (We've used a vinculum, a fancy term for the horizontal dividing line, throughout, in order to avoid confusion.)

Lastly, with the division line there is one assumed rule—everything above or below a horizontal division line is inside assumed brackets. So the expression $\frac{x + 1}{x - 3}$ could be written explicitly as $\frac{(x + 1)}{(x - 3)}$.

This is by no means a definitive list of the order of operations. In computer science there is a much larger list of operations and the corresponding order in which they are carried out. In mathematics we also have many more operations that can be performed, such as factorials (see pages 124–5).

Turn to pages 124–5 for information on factorials.

Exercise 1

Takin' Care of BEDMAS

THE PROBLEM:

Bachman and Turner entered a contest to win a new overdrive transmission for the 1969 Camaro. As it turns out their names were drawn and they won. The only catch was that they had to answer two tricky questions before they could claim their prize. The questions were:

a) $3 \cdot 6(5 - 2^2)$

b) $5[(3^4 - 6 \cdot 7) \div 13 - 8] - 4 \cdot 9$

THE METHOD:

You could just start at the beginning and work through to the end, solving each part in the order that you come to it; however, that will not produce the correct solution. Both Turner and Bachman are smarter than this. They apply the rules of BEDMAS.

THE SOLUTION:

Turner takes on the first question. Following the rules of BEDMAS, he has to evaluate inside the brackets. This has two operations: a subtraction and an exponent. Again, according to BEDMAS, the exponent ranks higher, therefore it's done first: $2^2 = 4$ giving us $3 \cdot 6(5 - 4)$.

Next we do the subtraction inside the brackets $5 - 4 = 1$ giving us $3 \cdot 6(1)$.

Now the only operation left is multiplication. Note that even though there is no multiplication sign, 6(1) is another representation of multiplication. So we perform the operation from left to right, giving an answer of 18.

Bachman takes on the second question, which is more complicated than the first expression as it has nested brackets. To solve this, we evaluate the brackets from the inside out.

First we focus on the "soft" brackets: $(3^4 - 6 \cdot 7)$. The exponent is the highest operation so it goes first: $3^4 = 81$, giving us $(81 - 6 \cdot 7)$.

Next we do the multiplication: $6 \cdot 7 = 42$, which gives us $(81 - 42)$ followed by the subtraction $(81 - 42)$ giving us (39).

The soft bracket is now complete and we place the result back within the larger expression to give us:

$$5[(39) \div 13 - 8] - 4 \cdot 9$$

Now we evaluate inside the "hard" brackets, doing the division first, $39 \div 13 = 3$, to give:

$$5[3 - 8] - 4 \cdot 9$$

Next we evaluate the subtraction inside the brackets, $3 - 8 = -5$. This gives us:

$$5(-5) - 4 \cdot 9$$

Then performing the multiplication from left to right gives:

$$-25 - 36$$

Finally the subtraction is performed for a solution of −61.

So Bachman and Turner won their overdrive transmission because they were takin' care of BEDMAS.

EXPRESSIONS, EQUALITIES, AND INEQUALITIES

Before we look too closely at equalities and inequalities, we need to understand the terminology. An expression is a collection of numbers and variables that can sometimes be simplified—it has neither an equals nor an inequality sign in it. An equation always includes an equals sign, while an inequation has an inequality sign where the equals sign would normally be.

One example of an expression is:

$$\frac{(3x - 4) + 5}{5x}$$

While an example of an equation is:

$$3x - 5 = 13$$

And an example of an inequation is:

$$3(x + 2) \leq 2x + 5$$

When it comes to inequalities: $>$ means "greater than"; $\geq$ means "greater than or equal to"; $<$ means "less than"; and $\leq$ means "less than or equal to."

Inequalities might seem odd, but we meet them all the time in everyday life, for example, when we're thinking about maximums and minimums.

Inequalities on a Number Line

Because inequalities have an infinite number of solutions, we often represent them on a number line. If we put $x \leq 3$ on a number line there would be a dot at three and the number line to the left would be shaded (see below). This represents all the values that make the inequality true. If we put $x > -2$ on a number line it would be a hollow dot at minus two, and the number line to the right would be shaded. A solid dot is used when the number forms part of the solution, in other words, when we use $\leq$ or $\geq$; while a hollow dot is used when the number is not part of the solution, in other words, when we use $<$ or $>$.

For example, $3x - 5$ is an expression; and it's one that we can't really do much with. Now, inserting an equals sign with something on the other side makes it an

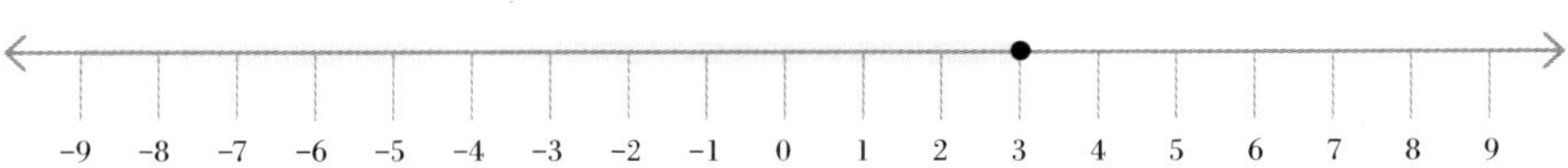

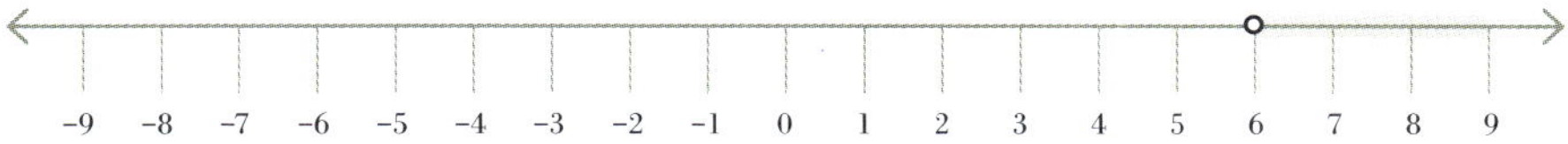

equation. To extend the example above, $3x - 5 = 13$ is an equation, so we can set about finding its solution, which is $x = 6$. Meanwhile, $3x - 5 > 13$ is an inequation which can also be solved. The solution is $x > 6$.

So, the equality generates a discrete solution: x is six and nothing else. On the other hand, the inequality generates a range of solutions, x could be seven, eight, or 6.000001, in fact anything greater than six. For an inequality there are an infinite number of solutions, and this is often expressed on a number line by shading to the right of the six (see above). Notice the six has a hollow circle above it, because a hollow dot signifies that it's not included in the solution.

Changing Direction

There's a common stumbling block with inequations, and the next example demonstrates this. Suppose that Sam and Dave made a deal with the Devil: in exchange for fame, one of them will have to give up his soul. The Devil gives them a task and whoever gets it right saves his soul. The task is to solve $-3x > 15$.

Sam and Dave both solve it, but in different ways. Sam divides both sides by −3 and gets $x > -5$. Dave, however, moves the $-3x$ to the right and the 15 over to the left to get $-15 > 3x$. Then Dave divides by 3 to give $-5 > x$. So Sam has numbers greater than −5 while Dave has numbers less than −5.

Who's right? Let's plug some numbers into the original equation to find out. If Sam is right then −4 should work; but it doesn't, and we get $12 > 15$. For Dave −6 should work. When we plug it in we get $18 > 15$, which is true. Dave wins and remains the soul man.

This demonstrates an important and often forgotten rule for inequalities: when multiplying or dividing by a negative number the direction of the inequality must switch.

GIVE US A SIGN

Although many of our mathematical symbols and notations are standardized today, many are not. In the past even fewer were standardized. The = sign was introduced in 1557 by Robert Recorde, a Welsh doctor and mathematician. The symbols > and < were first introduced in a book by Thomas Harriot, an English mathematician, in 1631, some ten years after his death; although his editor is credited for the notation. Interestingly, Harriot was also implicated in the famous plot to blow up the English parliament: "Remember, remember the fifth of November..." Then, over a hundred years later, in 1734, the symbols ≥ and ≤ were introduced by the French mathematician Pierre Bouguer.

Exercise 2

Solving Equations: The Basics

THE PROBLEMS:

Let's brush up on our basics by solving the following for x:

a) $x + 3 = 5$

b) $2x = 8$

c) $3x - 5 = 7$

d) $\frac{2}{3}x = 8$

e) $\frac{2}{3}(x - 6) = 8$

f) $\frac{2}{3}(x - 6) = 8(x + 3)$

THE METHOD:

To solve we perform opposite operations to isolate x. Generally speaking, the approach people take is often the same, but as the equations become more complicated the "routes" begin to vary. I follow an approach that works for me; you may choose a different route. As long as we end up at the same place, let's just be happy we got there.

THE SOLUTIONS:

a) In this problem, 3 is being added to x; therefore we subtract 3 from both sides (we perform the opposite operation):

$$x + 3 = 5$$
$$x + 3 - 3 = 5 - 3$$
$$x = 2$$

b) In this problem, 2 is being multiplied by x, therefore we divide both sides by 2:

$$2x = 8$$
$$2x \div 2 = 8 \div 2$$
$$x = 4$$

c) This one is more complicated, x is being multiplied by 3, and 5 is being subtracted:

$$3x - 5 = 7$$

Generally we remove the terms furthest from the variable first so we add 5 to both sides giving:

$$3x - 5 + 5 = 7 + 5 \text{ or}$$
$$3x = 12$$

Now x is being multiplied by 3, so we divide both sides by 3:

$$3x \div 3 = 12 \div 3 \text{ or}$$
$$x = 4$$

d) The fraction in front of the x can be viewed as a compound operation. x is being multiplied by 2 and divided by 3.

$$\tfrac{2}{3}x = 8$$

To remove the "÷ 3" we multiply by 3:

$$\tfrac{2}{3}x \cdot 3 = 8 \cdot 3 \text{ or}$$
$$2x = 8 \cdot 3 \text{ or}$$
$$2x = 24$$

To remove the "• 2" divide by 2:

$$2x \div 2 = 24 \div 2 \text{ or}$$
$$x = 12$$

e) This one has parentheses, so is slightly more complicated. I like to get rid of the parentheses early, so multiply both x and -6 by $\tfrac{2}{3}$:

$$\tfrac{2}{3}(x - 6) = 8$$
$$\tfrac{2}{3}x - 4 = 8$$

Add 4 to both sides to remove the "−4":

$$\tfrac{2}{3}x - 4 + 4 = 8 + 4 \text{ or}$$
$$\tfrac{2}{3}x = 12$$

Follow the previous example to get:

$$x = 18$$

f) This one has variables on both sides, and the dreaded parentheses. First we multiply to get rid of the parentheses:

$$\tfrac{2}{3}(x - 6) = 8(x + 3)$$
$$\tfrac{2}{3}x - 4 = 8x + 24$$

Again I diverge from others in that I like to get rid of the fractions early. I don't have anything against fractions, but many of my students do. So, I tell them that when you have an = sign you have power. You can do anything you want as long as you do it to both sides. In this case, I will multiply everything by 3:

$$\tfrac{2}{3}x \cdot 3 - 4 \cdot 3 = 8x \cdot 3 + 24 \cdot 3 \text{ or}$$
$$2x - 12 = 24x + 72$$

Now we will collect our xs on one side by subtracting $2x$ from both sides:

$$2x - 2x - 12 = 24x - 2x + 72 \text{ or}$$
$$-12 = 22x + 72$$

Now we subtract 72 to isolate the $22x$:

$$-12 - 72 = 22x + 72 - 72 \text{ or}$$
$$-84 = 22x$$

Now we divide by 22 to isolate x:

$$-84 \div 22 = 22x \div 22 \text{ or}$$
$$\tfrac{-84}{22} = x$$

This can be simplified to:

$$\tfrac{-42}{11} = x$$

Exercise 3

Solving Equations in Order

THE PROBLEM:

There are many applications that require the use of a square root; for example, accident investigators use a square-root equation to determine the speed a vehicle was traveling based on the length of its skid mark. Here we'll look at a more straightforward equation, to get used to the order of working through equations. So, find the value of x: $4 = 3 \cdot \sqrt{x + 7} - 5$

THE METHOD:

If you want to solve an equation you could just guess and check for a solution; but, depending on how lucky you are, this could take a while. A far better method is to use algebra.

Imagine you needed to get something out of a locked box in your attic. In front of the box is some junk you should have thrown out long ago. Past that is an old rug on top of the box; and lastly, inside the box is some more junk you need to move to get to what you want. If you wanted to get to the box, the first thing you would do is move the stuff in front of the box. Then you would remove the old rug. After that you would unlock the box. Finally, you would move the stuff in the box to get at your prize. The algebra problem above is just like that. You remove obstacles by performing opposite operations on both sides of the equation, one at a time until you have only the variable left, in this case x.

THE SOLUTION:

$$4 = 3 \cdot \sqrt{x+7} - 5$$

We need to get to x so the first thing to remove is the "– 5" by adding 5 to both sides. This is like removing the junk in front of the box, which gives:

$$9 = 3 \cdot \sqrt{x+7}$$

Next we need to get rid of the 3 by dividing both sides by 3. This is like shifting the rug on the box, which gives:

$$3 = \sqrt{x+7}$$

Now we remove the square root by squaring both sides. This is like unlocking the box, which gives:

$$9 = x + 7$$

Lastly we remove the "+ 7" by subtracting 7 from both sides. This is removing the junk in the box, which gives:

$$2 = x$$

And you're done. You've found the value of the variable, x.

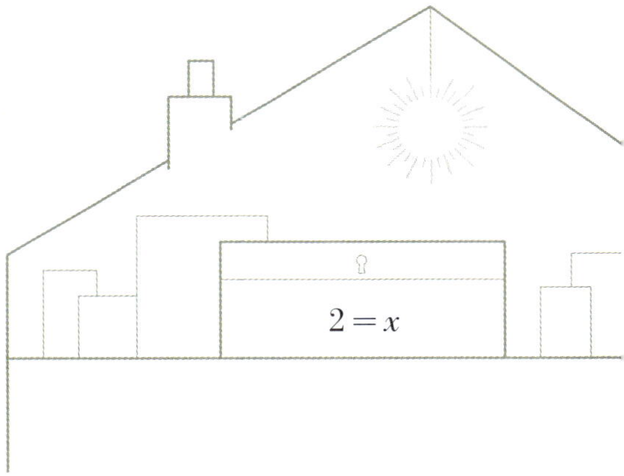

OPPOSITES ATTRACT

Much of mathematics is about opposite operations. Your calculator is even set up in pairs of opposite operations. Addition and subtraction are right next to each other. Multiplication and division are beside each other as well. Other functions have their opposites as "second" functions. Often the button that does squares is also the square-root button when "2nd" is pressed.

Performing an operation then its opposite straight after returns you to your original number. For example, if you take the sin(32°) you get 0.5299192642. If you then take the $\sin^{-1}$ (0.5299192642) you get 32°.

Exercise 14

Factoring Integers

THE PROBLEM:

John has 504 paving stones for an outdoor patio. He got the stones on the cheap because they were discontinued and he will not be able to get any more. Each stone measures 1 ft by 1 ft. John wants to use all the stones for his patio. What are all the possible dimensions for his patio?

THE METHOD:

Since John wants to use all the stones the dimensions of the patio will be number pairs that multiply to 504; *length* • *width* = *area*. Finding the number pairs which multiply to 504 is easy at first. The pairs 1 • 504 and 2 • 252 come to mind but it's possible you might miss a pair and I doubt that John wants a long strip for a patio. A more methodical approach is to find the prime factors first. This can be done by using factor trees or upside-down division. Once this is done, you have the prime factorization of:

$504 = 2 \cdot 2 \cdot 2 \cdot 3 \cdot 3 \cdot 7$ or
$504 = 2^3 \cdot 3^2 \cdot 7$

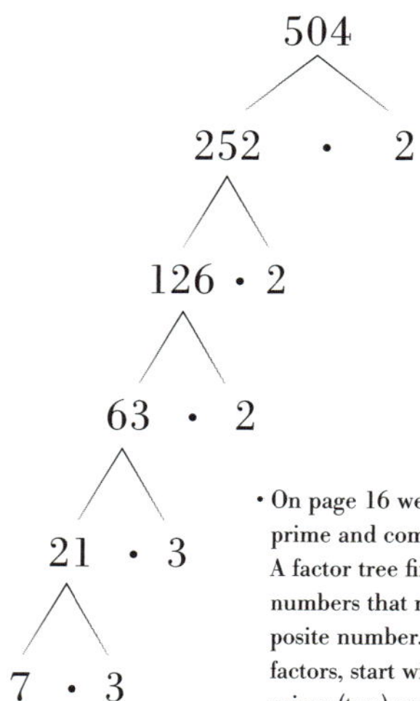

• On page 16 we talked about prime and composite numbers. A factor tree finds all the prime numbers that make up a composite number. To find the prime factors, start with the smallest prime (two) and divide the number by it. Continue dividing by two until the answer is not a whole number. Then divide by three, five, seven, and so on until you only have primes left.

This helps us determine the number of factors of 504.

Imagine you are at an ice-cream stand. They have four flavors, three types of cones, and two toppings. How many different combinations of ice cream, cones, and toppings—just one scoop, let's not get greedy—can you make? Well, the answer is:

$$4 \cdot 3 \cdot 2 = 24$$

The same is true for the factors of 504. You have four choices for the number of 2s (zero, one, two, or three 2s) in the factor, three choices for the number of 3s, and two choices for the number of 7s. So, including 1 and 504, there are 24 factors.

To clarify, 18 is a factor of 504 and it uses two 3s and a 2 from the prime factors of 504 ($3 \cdot 3 \cdot 2 = 18$). Its number pair—the other number which it multiplies with to make 504—is what remains from the prime factors $2 \cdot 2 \cdot 2 \cdot 3 \cdot 3 \cdot 7$, in other words $2 \cdot 2 \cdot 7$, which equals 28. Therefore:

$$18 \cdot 28 = 504$$

The factors in order are: 1, 2, 3, 4, 6, 7, 8, 9, 12, 14, 18, 21, 24, 28, 36, 42, 56, 63, 72, 84, 126, 168, 252, 504.

Next we have to pair them up so that each pair multiplies to 504. Now this looks daunting, but it's not a problem. If the numbers are written in order then all we need to do is combine one from the front of our list with one from the back, and keep doing this as we move toward the middle pair.

THE SOLUTION:

The number pairs are:

$1 \cdot 504$	$6 \cdot 84$	$12 \cdot 42$
$2 \cdot 252$	$7 \cdot 72$	$14 \cdot 36$
$3 \cdot 168$	$8 \cdot 63$	$18 \cdot 28$
$4 \cdot 126$	$9 \cdot 56$	$21 \cdot 24$

Therefore, John has twelve different options—there are twelve number pairs above—for the dimensions of his patio.

THE POWER OF POLYNOMIALS

Polynomials are important because they are used to model real-world problems. For example, degree-one polynomials (lines) are used in business for optimization problems (see pages 120–1), while degree-two polynomials (quadratics) are used to model problems including those involving gravity. Higher-degree polynomials are often used to model complex systems such as the economy.

What Is a Polynomial?

First let's introduce some terminology: a polynomial is a collection of terms. In elementary mathematics a "term" is a collection of variables raised to exponents and multiplied by a coefficient. An example of a term is $3x^2$ where 3 is the coefficient, x is the variable, and ^{2} is the exponent. Another example of a term would be $5xy^3$; where 5 is the coefficient, x and y are the variables, and ^{1} and ^{3} are the exponents. Note that although there is no exponent on the x it's implied that there is a ^{1} there.

There is, however, a restriction on the terms that can be included in polynomials: the exponents must be whole numbers. The whole number set is $\{0, 1, 2, 3, \ldots\}$, which does not include fractions, negative numbers, or irrational numbers. This means that terms like $4x^{\frac{1}{2}}$, $2\sqrt{x}$, and $\frac{5}{x^2}$ cannot be terms in a polynomial because the exponents on x are not whole numbers—the first is a fraction, the second square root is actually a fractional exponent, and the third is really a negative exponent.

Naming Polynomials

Polynomials can be defined by the number of terms in them: a polynomial of one term is called a monomial; one with two terms is a binomial; and one with three terms is a trinomial. When we get higher than that we just call them polynomials ("poly" meaning many).

Meanwhile, the degree of a polynomial is based on the term with the highest sum of exponents. For example, the expression $3x^2 - 4x + 5$ is a trinomial of degree two, because the highest exponent is a ^{2}. Likewise, $3x^2y^2 - 4xy + 5$ is a trinomial of degree four because there are three terms (so trinomial) and the first term has two squares, so the sum of the exponents is four (degree four).

Polynomials are very important in algebra. Firstly, polynomials of degree zero are just numbers—let's face it, we wouldn't get far without numbers. Polynomials of degree one (or linear functions) have been used to solve problems going back centuries (the equations solved on pages 28–9 were linear equations). Degree-two polynomials (or quadratic functions) were studied by ancient Babylonian, Greek, Indian, and Arab mathematicians and are used in most branches of science, engineering, mathematics, and economics. The Babylonians used tables of squares (quadratics) to solve multiplication problems. They used the formula:

$$ab = \frac{(a + b)^2 - (a - b)^2}{4}$$

This allowed them to look up sums and differences in the table and divide by four. As an example 12 • 8 would be:

$$\frac{20^2 - 4^2}{4}$$

In this case 20^2 and 4^2 would be found in a table, and plugged in as:

$$\frac{400 - 16}{4}$$

This can be simplified to:

$$\frac{384}{4}$$

Which reduces to 96.

A Brief History of Polynomials

Polynomials have been studied for many years; as we've mentioned earlier, solutions to quadratics (degree-two polynomials) stretch as far back as the ancient Babylonians.

The ancient Greek mathematician Euclid (see pages 54–5) solved quadratics with a purely geometrical approach around 300 BCE; but it was around a thousand years later when the Indian mathematician Brahmagupta (see pages 78–9) gave an almost modern approach to solving quadratics.

Later, in sixteenth-century Italy, the cubic and quartic equations (polynomials of degrees three and four) were the subject of some serious mathematical one-upmanship. Then, in 1824, Niels Abel (see below) proved that there is no general solution to polynomial equations of degree five.

NIELS ABEL

Born in Norway in 1802, Niels Henrik Abel spent a good portion of his life in poverty; but, luckily for him his mathematics teacher recognized his talent and helped support him through his higher education. He graduated from university in 1822, and just two years later he published his most notable work, which proved that there is no general solution to a polynomial equation of degree five.

In recognition of his work, the Norwegian government sponsors the Abel Prize, which some call the "Nobel Prize for mathematics," as there is no Nobel Prize in the field.

Exercise

5 Multiplying Polynomials

THE PROBLEMS:

a) Multiply the monomial by the binomial $2x(3x - 4)$

b) Multiply the two binomials $(2x - 3)(4x + 5)$

c) Multiply the two trinomials $(x^2 - 3x + 4)(x^2 + 2x + 1)$

THE METHOD

When multiplying polynomials we must make sure that all the terms from one polynomial are multiplied by all the terms in the other polynomial. For problem "a" we have a monomial (which has a single term) multiplied by a binomial (which has two terms).

This is like a single person introducing themselves to a couple—she would shake both people's hands. Therefore there are two multiplications. Two binomials—as in problem "b"—are like two couples. The first person from couple one shakes hands with both members of couple two, giving us two multiplications. Then the second person from couple one shakes hands with both members of couple two, giving us two more multiplications. This gives us a total of four handshakes or multiplications. The two trinomials—as in problem "c"—are like two couples, each with a child. Once everyone has shaken hands you'll have a total of nine handshakes, or multiplications.

a) For this problem you just multiply both terms of the binomial by the single term of the monomial:

$$2x(3x - 4) = 6x^2 - 8x$$

b) For this problem we have to "foil"—a mnemonic to make sure you remember all four of the multiplications you need to do: Firsts, Outers, Inners, and Lasts.

$$(2x - 3)(4x + 5) = 8x^2 + 10x - 12x - 15$$

Now we collect the "like terms," $10x$ and $-12x$ (see box), to give:

$$= 8x^2 - 2x - 15$$

Turn to pages 136–7 for information on the binomial theorem.

c) For the final problem we use the "horsey method," clip, clip, clip, clop, clop, clop, plop, plop, plop. Here's how to clean up with the horsey method:

$$(x^2 - 3x + 4)(x^2 + 2x + 1) = x^4 + 2x^3 + 1x^2 - 3x^3 - 6x^2 - 3x + 4x^2 + 8x + 4$$

"Clip, clip, clip," goes the first term in the first trinomial, as it multiplies all three terms in the second trinomial; then "clop, clop, clop" and "plop, plop, plop," go the second and third terms as they do the same.

Now we collect the like terms: $-3x$ and $8x$; $1x^2$, $-6x^2$, and $4x^2$; and $2x^3$ and $-3x^3$ (there are no like terms for x^4 or 4), to give:

$$x^4 - x^3 - x^2 + 5x + 4$$

THE SOLUTIONS

a) $2x(3x - 4) = 6x^2 - 8x$

b) $(2x - 3)(4x + 5) = 8x^2 - 2x - 15$

c) $(x^2 - 3x + 4)(x^2 + 2x + 1)$
$= x^4 - x^3 - x^2 + 5x + 4$

WHAT ARE LIKE TERMS?

Basically, "like terms" are terms that have the same type and number of variables. As an example, $6x^2$ and $8x^2$ are like terms; they both have two x variables.

However, $6x^2$ and $8x$ are not like terms. They both have x variables, but the first has two while the second only has one.

Now, $6y^2$ and $8x^2$, though both squares, are not like terms because they are different variables: y and x.

Lastly, $6xy^2$ and $8x^2y$, though containing the same variables, do not contain the same number of each variable and are not like terms. The first has an x variable and two y variables while the second has two x variables and one y variable.

TALKING TRIGONOMETRY

The word trigonometry comes from two Greek words *trigōnon* (triangle) and *metron* (measure), to measure the triangle. Its development spans all cultures, mostly due to the connection between trigonometry, astronomy, and navigation, and it still has many uses today—for example, in surveying and mapping.

The Babylonians

Around three millennia ago, the ancient Babylonians had a form of trigonometry, and it's from them that we take the idea of 360° in a circle. They also gave us sixty minutes in a degree and sixty seconds in a minute. That is to say, when you have 7.5° it can be written 7° 30', which reads "seven degrees thirty minutes." It's also the route of having sixty minutes in an hour and sixty seconds in a minute. All because the Babylonian number system was base-sixty (sexagesimal) and six sixties were a full circle.

The Greeks

The Greeks also worked with advanced trigonometry. Euclid (see pages 54–5) and Archimedes (see pages 58–9) developed theorems, albeit via geometry, which have trigonometric equivalents. It should be noted that the trigonometry of the ancient Greek world looked different from the trigonometry of today, as theirs was based on "chords" of circles—lines from edge to edge.

The first trigonometric table is thought to have been compiled by the second-century BCE mathematician and astronomer, Hipparchus of Nicaea, and

SIMILAR TRIANGLES

"Similar" triangles are those that have the same three angles in common. Though the triangles can be of varying sizes, the ratio of their corresponding sides will remain constant. Therefore, if we know that *A* is twice as long as *a*, then the value of *B* will be twice *b*, and *C* will be twice *c*.

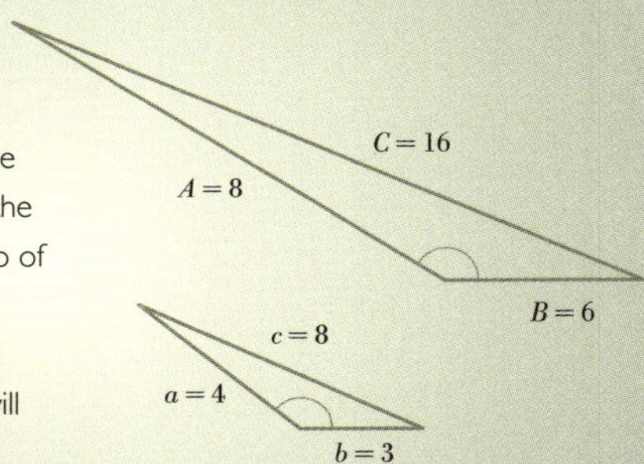

some call him the "father of trigonometry." The table was developed to aid in solving triangles, and Hipparchus is also credited with introducing the Greeks to the idea of 360° in a circle.

Somewhat later, Menelaus of Alexandria (c. 70–130 CE) wrote on spherical trigonometry, and the astronomer and geographer Ptolemy (c. 85–165 CE) furthered Hipparchus's work in his thirteen-volume *Almagest*.

Indians and Persians

The Indian mathematician Aryabhata (476–550 CE) developed the ratios for sine and cosine (see box) that most closely resemble our modern forms. His work also contains the earliest surviving sine tables. In the seventh century the Indian mathematician Bhaskara produced a fairly accurate formula (for use with radians not degrees) to calculate the sine of x without a table:

$$\sin x \approx \frac{16x\,(\pi - x)}{5\pi^2 - 4x(\pi - x)}, \quad (0 \le x \le \tfrac{\pi}{2})$$

These ideas migrated west through Persia. Al-Khwarizmi (see pages 86–7) produced trigonometric tables for sine, cosine, and tangent in the ninth century. A century later, Islamic mathematicians were using all six ratios and had tables for quarter-degree increments accurate to eight decimals. In the eleventh century Al-Jayyani, who was born in Cordoba, Spain, produced work containing formulas for right-angled triangles which likely influenced European mathematics.

SIX OF A KIND

The six trigonometric ratios refer to the ratios (fractions) of the three sides of a right-angled triangle. This means that if you know certain angles and side lengths you can use them to determine the values of those you don't. All you need to know is which ratio to use:

sine θ = opposite ÷ hypotenuse
cosine θ = adjacent ÷ hypotenuse
tangent θ = opposite ÷ adjacent
cosecant θ = hypotenuse ÷ opposite
(note this is the reciprocal of sine)
secant θ = hypotenuse ÷ adjacent
(note this is the reciprocal of cosine)
cotangent θ =adjacent ÷ opposite
(note this is the reciprocal of tangent)

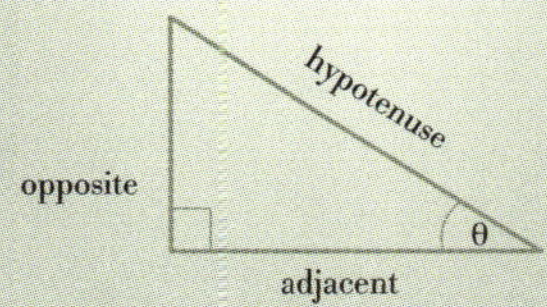

Trigonometry Today

Today there are a huge number of practical applications for trigonometry. As well as surveying and mapping, which we've already mentioned, it's put to use in navigation. For example, both the traditional sextant that sailors used to gauge their position on the world's oceans and the more modern invention of satellite navigation systems use trigonometry. It's also used on a more theoretical basis to model financial markets among many other areas.

Exercise 6

Trigonometry: To Fell a Tree

THE PROBLEM:

A man has to take down a tree on his property. It's close to two fences that he wants to avoid. In which direction(s) can he safely fell the tree without endangering either of the fences? Note, felling the tree in the opposite direction is not an option.

THE METHOD

This is a real problem that confronted me one summer. I wanted to take a dead tree down before the winter storms did, and I wanted to have control over where it fell.

My first task was to find out the height of the tree. One option was to climb it with a tape measure, but I'm not that brave or stupid. The second, somewhat safer, option was to make a clinometer and use trigonometry. A clinometer sounds impressive, but it's just a device for measuring inclines. They're easy to make: you just need a protractor, string, and a weight to tie to the string. Using a laser level—to keep myself roughly horizontal—I walked to the back fence and looked along the protractor to the top of the tree. I found the angle to be between 50° and 55°. Knowing the angle and the length of the base (the distance from the tree to the fence was 16 m), I used the tangent ratio (see box right):

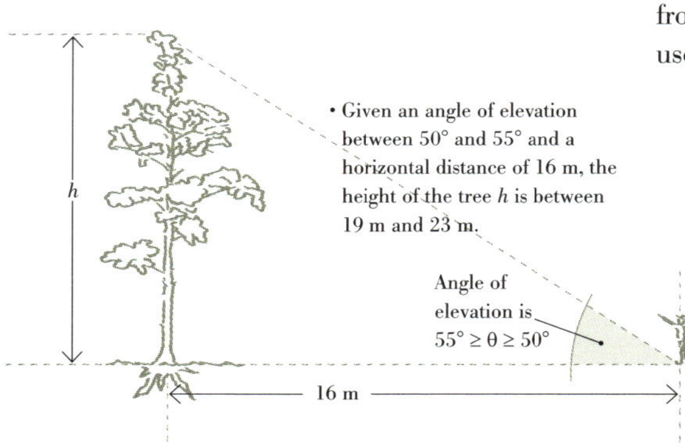

$$\tan\theta = \frac{opposite}{adjacent}$$

or

$$\tan 50 = \frac{height}{16}$$

This can be expressed as:

$$height = 16 \cdot \tan 50 = 19 \text{ m}$$

Repeated for 55°, the equation produced 23 m. I averaged these results out to give a height of 21 m. Task one done.

My second task was to determine my level of error for felling the tree. Now that I had the height of the tree, it could represent the hypotenuse of three triangles on the ground. Using the inverse cosine function (see right) I could determine the value of θ_1:

$$\cos^{-1}\frac{16}{21} = \theta_1$$

or $\theta_1 = 40°$. This angle will be the same for triangle two because they are congruent (the same). Using the same approach the value of $\theta_3 = 36°$.

SOH CAH TOA

How do you know which ratio to use and when? Well, it depends on which sides you have values for, and there is a neat mnemonic to help you remember:

$$\sin \theta = \frac{opposite}{hypotenuse}$$

$$\cos \theta = \frac{adjacent}{hypotenuse}$$

$$\tan \theta = \frac{opposite}{adjacent}$$

Just remember SOH CAH TOA. Also, to remember when to use the inverse trig function I like to say that "angles are shifty dudes"—this reminds me that when I want to find an angle I use the shift or "2nd" button to find it on a calculator.

THE SOLUTION

Now I knew all the angles it was easy to determine the directions I could fell the tree. Toward the corner post I had an arc of 14° to work with, quite a narrow angle, but maybe more if I overestimated the height. Note: the tree came down safely with no damage.

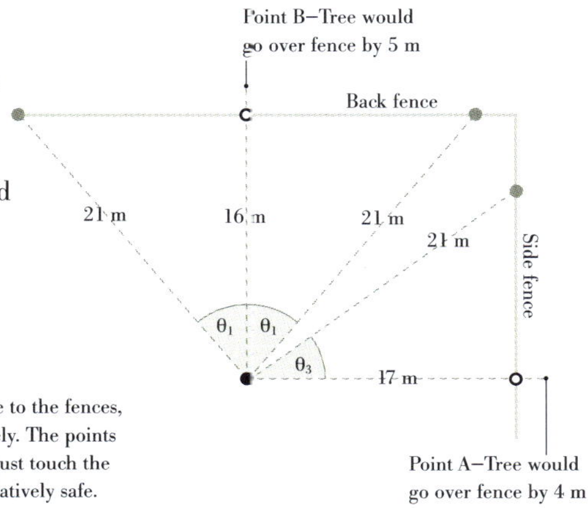

• Points A and B are the shortest distances from the tree to the fences, and the tree would go over by 4 m and 5 m respectively. The points where the distance is 21 m are where the tree would just touch the fence. This left an arc in which felling the tree was relatively safe.

Chapter

2

Ancient Greece

When people think about the history of mathematics they tend to think about ancient Greece. After all, we take many of our mathematical symbols from the Greek alphabet: we've already met π and φ (the golden ratio). And if you ask anyone to name a famous mathematician, the chances are they'll choose Pythagoras, Archimedes, or some other long-dead Greek. To a certain extent this familiarity exposes a Western bias in our thinking, but it does make ancient Greece a good place to start our journey into algebra.

Profile

Pythagoras

Pythagoras is often the first historical mathematician people are introduced to. Up until Pythagoras, mathematics is really quite nameless. Throughout most of our early years we learn about arithmetic, and it's not until we reach the Pythagorean theorem that we get a chance to put a face to the numbers. As it turns out Pythagoras is quite a good person to start with as he had a profound influence on mathematics.

Pythagoras of Samos was born about 570 BCE on the Greek island of that name, in the Aegean near Turkey. He's sometimes described as the first pure mathematician, studying mathematics as a theoretical pursuit not a practically applied discipline. This is important because making the intellectual leap from five apples, five people, five boats, and so on, to the abstract number five was a significant event, even if it's something we're now used to in our everyday lives.

Unlike many other historical figures, there are no primary sources for Pythagoras. Either his writings have been destroyed or Pythagoras did not write but rather had students record his thoughts. The secret nature of his group would have also contributed to the dearth of written material. Therefore all of our accounts of Pythagoras come from other sources, some that seem reasonable and others fantastic.

The Life of Pythagoras

What we know of the life of Pythagoras is quite detailed considering that we have to go back two and a half millennia. He spent his youth in Samos but traveled extensively with his father, Mnesarchus, a merchant from Tyre. Pythagoras visited Thales, a Greek philosopher, scientist, mathematician, and engineer by trade, in Miletus and attended lectures given by Anaximander, a student of Thales.

Pythagoras also traveled to Egypt, and during a war between Egypt and Persia, he was captured and taken to Babylon. Around 520 BCE, Pythagoras returned to Samos. Shortly thereafter he went to southern Italy and founded his Pythagorean school at Croton.

Pythagoras's group, the Pythagoreans, was a bit of a cult, mixing religion and mathematics. The group at Croton was in some ways a school, a monastery, and a brotherhood—although Pythagoras allowed women to join, so perhaps it was more a commune than a brotherhood. The Pythagoreans consisted of two groups. The first group, called the *mathematikoi*, lived with and were taught by Pythagoras. The group was required to live an ethical life, practice pacifism and study the "true nature of reality"—mathematics or numbers. The second group was the *akousmatikoi*, who lived in their own house and only attended the school during the day.

However, it wasn't all mathematics; the Pythagoreans also believed in the transmigration of souls and reincarnation, while one of the stranger rules the Pythagoreans followed was the abstinence of eating beans. I tell my students that if you wear a bed sheet all day you don't want to spend your time fluffing the sheets.

PYTHAGORAS AND MUSIC

Pythagoras and the Pythagoreans were very interested in music, being musicians as well as mathematicians. One story goes that Pythagoras was passing a blacksmith when he heard harmonious notes emanating from the shop. Upon inspection Pythagoras realized the notes were related to the size of the tool. Using simple fractions Pythagoras produced the notes that we know today. If you have a string and pluck it to produce a "C" then shorten the string to half its length and pluck again you will hear a "C," one octave up. A string shortened to half its length produces a frequency that is twice as big, in other words an octave higher.

Note	String Length
C	1
D	$\frac{8}{9}$
E	$\frac{4}{5}$
F	$\frac{3}{4}$
G	$\frac{2}{3}$
A	$\frac{3}{5}$
B	$\frac{8}{15}$
C	$\frac{1}{2}$

Pythagoras and Mathematics

Mathematically, the Pythagoreans are known for many things: the Pythagorean theorem, the mathematics of music, and the discovery of the square root of two. It should be noted that Pythagoras might not have been responsible for the development of all these ideas, but more likely the members of the group developed them. Given the secrecy surrounding the Pythagoreans and the communal nature of the group, it's hard to determine what work was Pythagoras's and what wasn't. (The Pythagorean theorem is discussed in detail on the following pages and the square root of two is mentioned in the section on irrational numbers.)

In 508 BCE the Pythagorean Society was attacked by Cylon, a noble from Croton. Pythagoras escaped to Metapontium and died around eight years later. After his death two distinct groups formed, one mathematical and one religious.

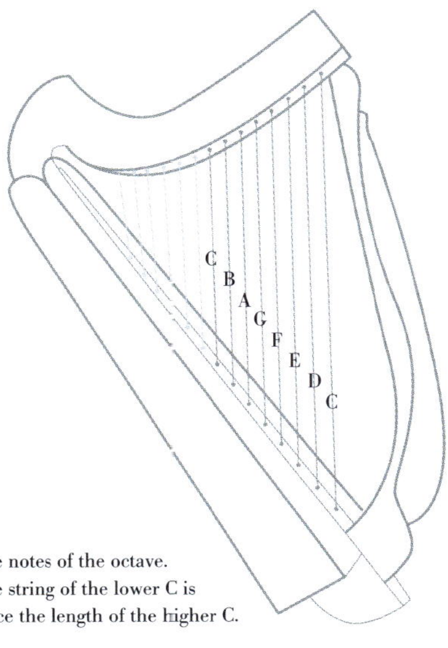

• The notes of the octave. The string of the lower C is twice the length of the higher C.

PYTHAGOREAN THEOREM

The Pythagorean theorem is one of the best-known pieces of mathematics—it's one of the few things people remember from school. The theorem also has many everyday applications.

The Pythagorean theorem states that given a right-angled triangle (below) the sum of squares of the two shorter sides equals the square of the longer side, or as the formula: $a^2 + b^2 = c^2$.

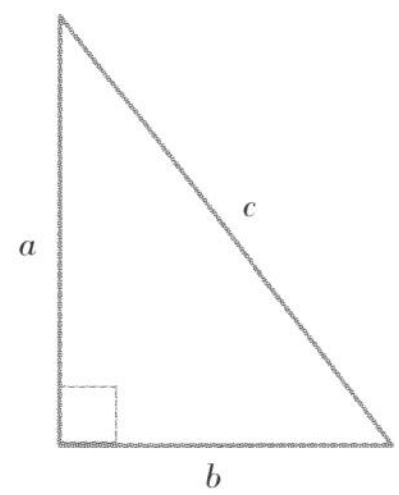

A Simple Proof

Though the formula is named after Pythagoras, the theorem was actually known to the Babylonians and Indians long before before his time. However, it's thought that Pythagoras, or perhaps one of the Pythagoreans, was the first to construct a proof of the theorem. So here is one of the many ways that it can be proved. The area of the large square is:

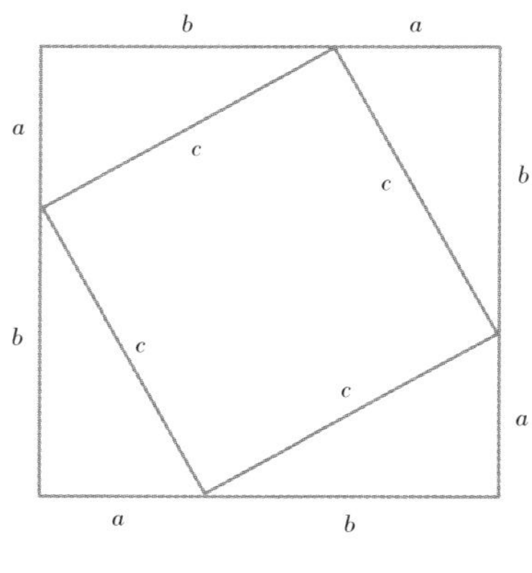

$$(a + b)^2 \text{ or } (a + b)(a + b)$$

After we "foil" this out (see page 34) and collect the like terms we have:

$$a^2 + 2ab + b^2$$

The area of the large square can also be determined by adding the areas of the four triangles and the smaller square of side length c. The area of the slanted square is c^2, and the area of one of the triangles is $\frac{1}{2}ab$. So the sum of the four triangles and the slanted square is:

$$4 \cdot \frac{1}{2}ab + c^2$$

This simplifies to $2ab + c^2$.

Now, since we are talking about the same square, the areas must be equal, therefore:

$$a^2 + 2ab + b^2 = 2ab + c^2$$

The $2ab$ that appears on both sides of the equation cancels itself out leaving:

$$a^2+b^2=c^2$$

A Common Use of the Theorem

In construction, the Pythagorean theorem is used to check how square a corner is, though I doubt workers go about saying: "Hold on while I apply the Pythagorean theorem to determine the angle of the corner." However, it's what they do, because a quick way to see if a corner is square (90°) is to measure down one wall three meters, down the other wall four meters, then measure the diagonal between these two points. If the diagonal is not five meters, then the walls are not square. You can extend down both walls by multiples of three and four to gain more accuracy.

Pythagorean Triples

This example using three, four, and five for the sides of a right-angled triangle is called a "Pythagorean triple." There are many Pythagorean triples including any multiple of three, four, and five; in fact, the aspect ratios (the ratio of length to height) of both regular (4:3 ratio) and widescreen (16:9 ratio) televisions are both part of Pythagorean triples. Here's the formula for determining them.

Given two whole numbers n and m such that n is greater than m:

$$a=n^2-m^2$$
$$b=2nm$$
$$c=n^2+m^2$$

So if $n=2$ and $m=1$ then:

$$a=2^2-1^2=4-1=3$$
$$b=2\cdot 2\cdot 1=4$$
$$c=2^2+1^2=4+1=5$$

Using different values of n and m you can create as many Pythagorean triples as you like.

The 3D Experience

One more interesting thing about the Pythagorean theorem is that it can be generalized to other dimensions. For those of us in the real world that means three dimensions.

As an example, say that Suzie is collecting little nick-nacks and plans to use a shoe box to store them. She sees a novelty pencil in a store, but needs to know if it will fit into the box before she buys it. Okay, so a normal person would just get on and buy it, but hey, don't knock Suzie—she's sensitive.

Luckily for us, Suzie knows the dimensions of the box: it's 18 cm wide, 28 cm long, and 11 cm high. She then applies the theorem to three dimensions or $a^2+b^2+c^2=d^2$ where a, b, and c are the width, length, and height and d is the diagonal. So Suzie has:

$$18^2+28^2+11^2=d^2$$

This becomes:

$$324+784+121=d^2 \text{ or } 1229=d^2$$

taking the square root of both sides we find that Suzie can get a 35 cm pencil.

RADICAL MATHEMATICS

"Radicals," or more specifically square roots, have been known for centuries. The Rhind Papyrus makes reference to square roots as long ago as c. 1650 BCE, but this is not surprising given that square roots are tied to the areas and diagonals of squares and rectangles; so temple construction would have required an understanding of them. In modern times they've all sorts of uses, such as allowing electrical engineers to calculate the average power dissipation in a circuit.

The Square Root of Two

The square root of two ($\sqrt{2}$) was a big deal to the Pythagoreans (see pages 44–5). The discovery that the square root of two was irrational really bothered them. To the Pythagoreans the world was all about numbers, and that meant rational numbers. The idea that a number could not be expressed as a fraction was inconceivable.

Legend has it that Hippasus of Metapontum, a disciple of Pythagoras, produced a proof of the irrationality of the square root of two. Because the Pythagoreans could not accept this, Hippasus was sentenced to death by drowning. An alternative story suggests that his discovery was made at sea, so he was simply thrown overboard. Who knows for sure? Maybe they just expelled him from the group, but it makes for a good story, and illustrates just how irrational people can get about numbers.

Another Famous Greek

Archimedes (see pages 58–9) had a very accurate estimate of the square root of three ($\sqrt{3}$), which he used in *Measurement of a Circle*, the same text in which he outlined his estimate for π.

Archimedes' estimate for $\sqrt{3}$ was $\frac{265}{153} < \sqrt{3} < \frac{1351}{780}$, or expressed in decimals $1.7320261 < \sqrt{3} < 1.7320512$. It's worth noting that the second figure is out by only 0.0000004, which is very close considering that Archimedes didn't have a calculator or a base-ten system to work with—multiplication and division using Greek numerals was very difficult. Some mathematical historians suggest that Archimedes used the Babylonian method.

The Babylonian method or Heron's method is an elegant iterative (repetitive) formula: Given $x_0 \approx \sqrt{S}$ the estimate root is found using:

$$x_{n+1} = \frac{1}{2}\left(x_n + \frac{S}{x_n}\right)$$

As an example we'll estimate the square root of three ($\sqrt{3}$). Note that $\sqrt{3}$ on a calculator is 1.732050808.

First we need a starting estimate: x_0. As we know the square root of four is two, we'll start there. It's too large, but the formula will help us work our way down to the right value. Substituting x_0 for x_n makes x_{n+1} equal to x_1.

$$x_1 = \frac{1}{2}\left(x_0 + \frac{S}{x_0}\right)$$

where $x_0 = 2$ and $S = 3$ (for $\sqrt{3}$)

$$x_1 = \frac{1}{2}\left(2 + \frac{3}{2}\right) = 1.75$$

Note that we already have the first two digits correct and we have a value for x_1, a better estimate for $\sqrt{3}$. Using $x_1 = 1.75$ we can now apply the formula again and get an even better estimate:

$$x_2 = \frac{1}{2}\left(x_1 + \frac{S}{x_1}\right)$$

Where $x_1 = 1.75$ and $S = 3$ (for $\sqrt{3}$)

$$x_2 = \frac{1}{2}\left(1.75 + \frac{3}{1.75}\right) = 1.7321$$

We've now found the first four digits of $\sqrt{3}$, and if we wanted we could continue this process to arrive at better and better estimates for the square root of three.

HERON OF ALEXANDRIA

Along with his method of determining square roots Heron of Alexandria (c. 10–70 CE) provided a neat way of finding the area of a non-right-angled triangle, using the formula:

$$area = \sqrt{s(s-a)(s-b)(s-c)}$$

where $s = \dfrac{a+b+c}{2}$

or in another form:

$$area = \frac{\sqrt{(a+b+c)(a+b-c)(b+c-a)(c+a-b)}}{4}$$

Here *a*, *b*, and *c* are the sides of the triangle, and s is its semi perimeter (half its perimeter). Though this formula looks ugly it's really quite nice. Moreover, because of the difficulties in doing calculations in ancient Greece, Heron's formula offered a much easier solution.

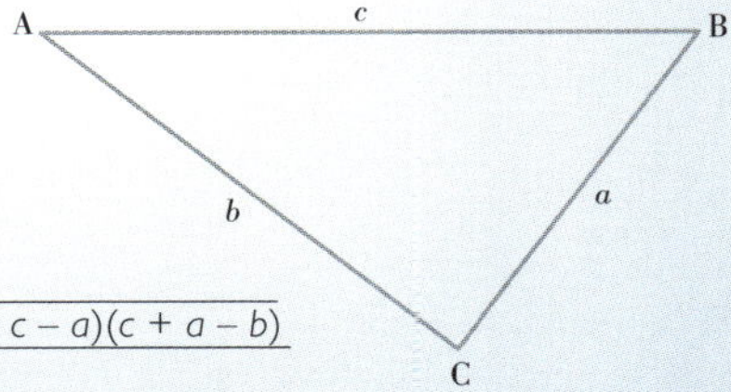

Exercise

7 Simplifying Radicals

THE PROBLEM:

Today, with the use of calculators, the values of square roots are easy to find. In the past it was more complicated and only some square roots were known to a high degree of accuracy. Fortunately, many square roots are multiples of base square roots such as $\sqrt{2}$, $\sqrt{3}$ and $\sqrt{5}$. Archie needs to find out the value of $\sqrt{180}$, but he does not have a calculator. He does, however, have a table with the values of the square roots of some primes. To find the value of $\sqrt{180}$, Archie needs to write the radical in simplest form.

THE METHOD

First, what is a "simplest form" radical? Simply put, it's a radical where all possible squares are removed from the radical. As an example, $2\sqrt{3}$ is equal to $\sqrt{12}$, but $2\sqrt{3}$ is the simplest form of the radical because $\sqrt{12}$ can be written as $\sqrt{4} \cdot \sqrt{3}$ where the $\sqrt{4}$ can be changed into a 2, giving us $2\sqrt{3}$.

This might seem hard, but there are a few tricks. The standard approach to simplifying radicals is to find perfect squares within the radical. Perfect squares are numbers like 1, 4, 9, 16, 25, 36, and so on. We want perfect squares because the square roots they give are nice natural numbers. For example:

$$\sqrt{4} = 2 \text{ and } \sqrt{25} = 5$$

This can be done by using a factor tree or upside-down division. For this problem both 4 and 9 go into 180 so in a factored form it would look like:

$$\sqrt{4 \cdot 9 \cdot 5}$$

This can be rewritten as $\sqrt{4} \cdot \sqrt{9} \cdot \sqrt{5}$, and with $\sqrt{4} = 2$ and $\sqrt{9} = 3$ it can be further reduced to $2 \cdot 3 \cdot \sqrt{5}$ or $6\sqrt{5}$.

Another, and I think better, approach is to find all the prime factors of the number. Again we would use a factor tree or upside-down division. So for 180 the prime factors are 2 • 2 • 3 • 3 • 5, so the radical would look like:

$$\sqrt{2 \cdot 2 \cdot 3 \cdot 3 \cdot 5}$$

and we would remove pairs of primes.

The reason we remove pairs is that this is a square root. If we had a cube root we would remove groups of three. We use this method when we "jail break."

Jail breaking is a method I use to remember how to simplify radicals. What do we do with radicals? We send them to jail. What do they want to do? Break out of jail. So the first step in breaking out of jail is to break the prison population into its cliques (prime factors), because jailbirds only trust their own. If they're going to break out of jail (a square-root prison), two numbers need to work together. As one number goes over the top, it distracts the guards and gets shot. As this is happening, the other number tunnels free.

So, in our example, a 2 and 3 die as they try to go over the top, but their buddies make it through to the outside. The 5 gets left kicking its heels in jail because it has no partner to distract the guards.

THE SOLUTION

This gives a solution of $(3 \cdot 2)\sqrt{5}$ or $6\sqrt{5}$. Now that Archie has simplified the radical, all he needs to do is multiply the $\sqrt{5}$ by 6 or (2.236) • (6) to get 13.416.

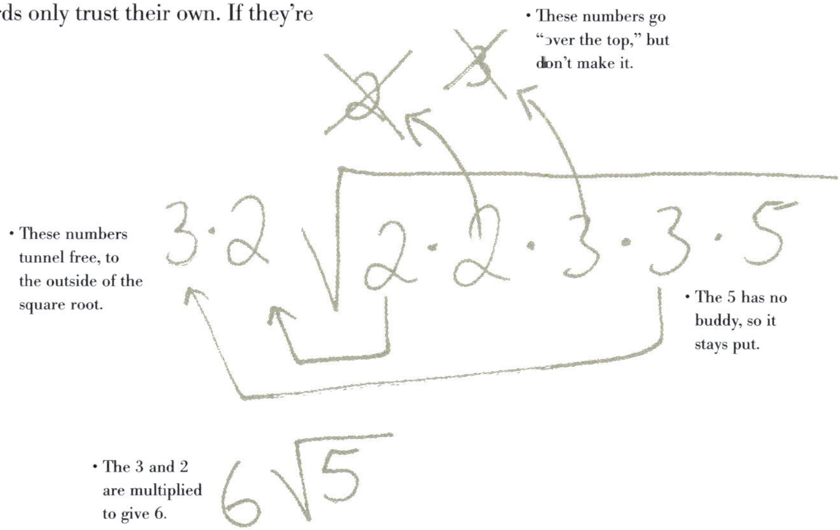

Profile

Plato

Even if many people don't know exactly what he did, the name of Plato is known to most people in the Western world. He is one of the big guns of philosophy, but is also renowned in mathematical circles, not so much for any advances, but more for his attitude toward the subject. Plato was a torch bearer of mathematics; and through him the mathematics of Pythagoras and his followers was passed on to Euclid (see pages 54–5) and Archimedes (see pages 58–9).

Plato was born in Athens c. 427 BCE. The son of wealthy parents, he was afforded a solid education in his youth. However, at the time he was growing up, the Peloponnesian War was waxing and waning as Athens and its empire struggled for supremacy against Sparta and its allies in the Peloponnesian League. Plato started his military service in 409 BCE (aged 18) and ended it in 404 BCE.

During these years it's almost certain that Plato was a follower of Socrates, as Plato makes mention of him in his *Dialogues*, and Socrates was also a friend of his uncle, Charmides. In fact, the arrest, trial, and execution of Socrates had a significant impact on Plato, and after the execution in 399 BCE he left Greece for Egypt, Sicily, and Italy.

Plato and Pythagoras

When in Italy, Plato learned of the works of the Pythagoreans, and from these developed his ideas on reality. The Pythagoreans are considered the first group to study mathematics as an intellectual pursuit, helping to separate the world of mathematics from the "real world," and this affected Plato greatly.

Plato considered mathematical objects to be perfect forms, which cannot be created in the real world. In *Phaedo*, Plato talks of objects in the real world trying to be like their perfect forms. As an example, a line in mathematics has length but no width, therefore it's impossible to draw a true line in reality, because a line on a page requires some width in order to be seen. A perfect line also continues forever, which is just as impossible to draw. Of course, we can draw lines with arrows on them to represent the infinite direction, but this is just a crude representation.

These ideas may seem sensible to us now, but we must remember that all those years ago the Greeks did not have the concept or mathematical symbol for zero.

Plato and the Academy

Plato returned to Athens in 387 BCE and founded the academy where he worked until his death in 347 BCE. The academy was devoted to research into philosophy, science, and mathematics.

"Arithmetic has a very great and elevating effect, compelling the soul to reason about abstract number, and rebelling against the introduction of visible or tangible objects into the argument." ***The Republic***

Though very fond of mathematics, Plato did not advance mathematical thought, though the ideas of Pythagoras continued through him, and his reverence of mathematics extended to his students. This makes Plato a very important link in the chain of Greek mathematics. In fact, Plato felt that mathematics was so important that the words "Let no one unversed in geometry enter here" or "Let no one ignorant of mathematics enter here" (depending on your translation) were written above the entrance to the academy. In fact, in *The Republic* Plato states that one must study the five mathematical disciplines: arithmetic, plane geometry, solid geometry, astronomy, and music, before moving on to the study of philosophy.

Turn to pages 52–3 for information on Platonic solids.

Actually, there is some mathematics attached to Plato: the Platonic solids. Though they are named after him these five shapes with neat properties—the tetrahedron, cube, octahedron, dodecahedron, and icosahedron—were known to many before Plato's time. (They are, discussed in more depth on pages 52–3.)

Plato's Academy continued until 529 CE when the Roman Emperor Justinian had it closed down.

"Those who have a natural talent for calculation are generally quick-witted at every other kind of knowledge; and even the dull, if they have had an arithmetical training, although they may derive no other advantage from it, always become much quicker than they would have been." ***The Republic***

Major Works

- **The Republic**
  Plato's best-known work deals with the ideal society, ideal rulers, and forms of government. Plato also talks of imperfect representations of perfect mathematical objects.

- **Phaedo**
  Describes Socrates' death and discusses the afterlife, giving four arguments for the soul's immortality. It also talks about perfect forms and imperfect representations of them.

- **Timaeus**
  Contains a construction that gives the Platonic solids the characteristics of the elements earth, fire, air, and water as well as the universe (see pages 52–3).

PLATONIC SOLIDS

The Platonic solids, as well as the Archimedean solids shown on pages 60–1, are nice curiosities of three-dimensional geometry. They can be seen in all sorts of interesting places, from such everyday objects as dice, to the shapes of molecules (methane is a tetrahedron) and even viruses (the herpes virus is an icosahedron).

The five Platonic solids are all regular and are the tetrahedron, hexahedron (cube), octahedron, dodecahedron, and icosahedron. This familiar-looking set of shapes is named after Plato (see pages 50–1), though it's very unlikely that he discovered them.

Sources suggest that the Pythagoreans (see pages 42–3) were aware of the regular tetrahedron, hexahedron, and dodecahedron. However, it's likely that the discovery of the regular octahedron and the regular icosahedron belongs to Theaetetus (417–369 BCE), a Greek

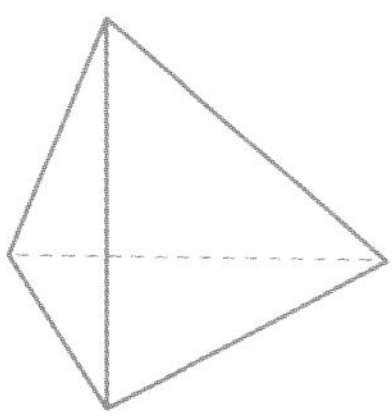

TETRAHEDRON
4 vertices, 6 edges, and 4 faces

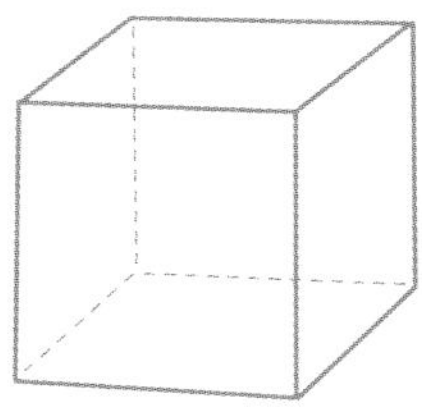

HEXAHEDRON (CUBE)
8 vertices, 12 edges, and 6 faces

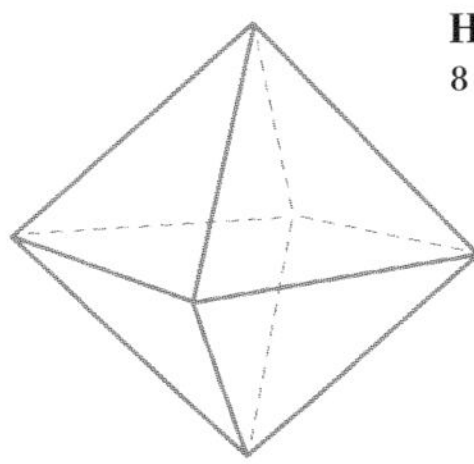

OCTAHEDRON
6 vertices, 12 edges, and 8 faces

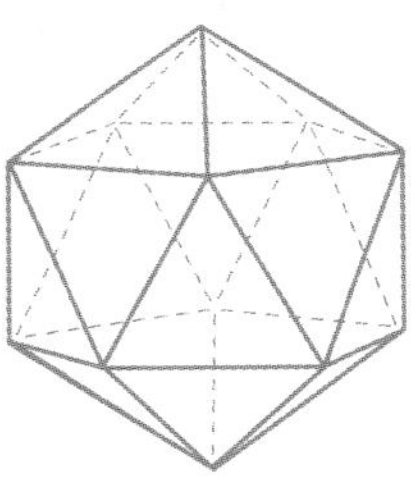

ICOSAHEDRON
12 vertices, 30 edges, and 20 faces

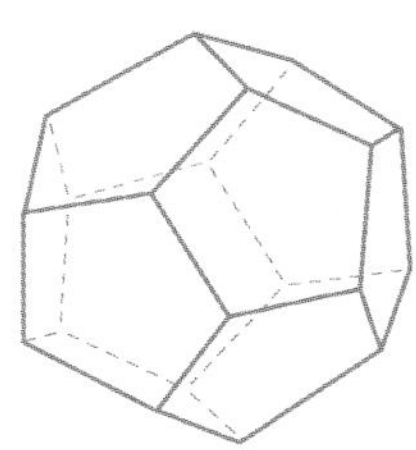

DODECAHEDRON
20 vertices, 30 edges, and 12 faces

ABOUT FACES

With the Platonic solids there is also a relationship between the faces, edges, and vertices. Looking at the tetrahedron, it has four faces, four vertices (where the sides come together at a point), and six edges. The cube has six faces, eight vertices, and twelve edges. Look at the final column and you'll see a neat symmetry to the relationships between the faces, vertices, and edges of all five Platonic solids.

Polyhedra	Faces (*F*)	Vertices (*V*)	Edges (*E*)	*F + V – E*
Tetrahedron	4	4	6	4 + 4 – 6 = 2
Hexahedron	6	8	12	6 + 8 – 12 = 2
Octahedron	8	6	12	8 + 6 – 12 = 2
Dodecahedron	12	20	30	12 + 20 – 30 = 2
Icosahedron	20	12	30	20 + 12 – 30 = 2

mathematician who studied under Plato and is the central character in two of Plato's *Dialogues*. This idea is also supported in Book XIII of Euclid's *Elements*.

It's also believed that Theaetetus gave the first proof that there are only five such shapes, at least in the case of three-dimensional objects.

Properties of the Platonic Solids

First it's necessary to define what makes a Platonic solid. To be a Platonic solid an object must have congruent (equal) faces; these faces must only intersect at the edges; and the same number of faces must meet at each vertex (or point). What this really means is that no matter which face is down (or at the bottom) the shape will look the same. This makes the Platonic solids fair, and that's why they're used as dice. The regular hexahedron (cube) is the common six-sided dice, while the others are used in role-playing games and wargames. The interesting relationship between the faces, vertices, and edges is shown in the table above.

Meanwhile, Plato also attributed some less mathematically sound, but still fascinating, attributes to the Platonic solids. He married them to the classical elements of the ancient world, making the tetrahedron fire, the hexahedron earth, the octahedron air, and the icosahedron water. The fifth Platonic solid, the dodecahedron was given the role of arranging the constellations.

Profile

Euclid

Euclid of Alexandria is widely acclaimed as the father of geometry. His book, or collection of books, the *Elements* was the authoritative text on geometry for over two thousand years, and has been called the most successful textbook in the history of mathematics. The geometry we learn in school is Euclidian geometry. In fact, until the early nineteenth century, it was the only geometry. Euclidian geometry is one of the most enjoyable branches of mathematics to learn and teach.

"There is no royal road to geometry"

Euclid's Life

For someone who wrote one of the most influential books in mathematics, surprisingly little is know about Euclid. He was born around 325 BCE, though we don't know where. There is some suggestion that Euclid attended Plato's academy (see pages 50–1), though most likely after the death of Plato. And he is said to have been active and teaching in Alexandria during the reign of Ptolemy I, one of Alexander the Great's generals, who ruled Egypt from 323–283 BCE.

So little is known about Euclid that some speculate about whether he really existed or not. Three options have been presented: that Euclid did exist and wrote the books himself; that Euclid was a leader of a group of mathematicians who collectively wrote as Euclid (much like Pythagoras and the Pythagoreans); or that Euclid didn't exist

Other Works

- **DATA**
  Deals with the properties of figures which can be deduced when other properties are given.
- **ON DIVISION OF FIGURES**
  Looks at dividing figures into two or more equal parts.
- **CATOPTRICS**
  A work on the mathematical theory of mirrors.
- **PHAENOMENA**
  Deals with spherical astronomy.
- **OPTICS**
  Covers the mathematics of perspective.
- **CONICS (LOST)**
  A work on the conic sections (see page 91).
- **PSEUDARIA OR BOOK OF FALLACIES (LOST)**
  A text on errors in logic.

but was a group of mathematicians writing as Euclid. Assuming that Euclid was alive in the first place—and I do—he is thought to have died around 265 BCE.

Elements of Geometry

Elements is Euclid's big work; a collection of thirteen books dealing with geometry and number theory. A common misconception is that *Elements* is a book of Euclid's own discoveries; but this isn't true, as most of the mathematics in it were known before Euclid's time. Euclid's real accomplishment was to collect and organize the information, and provide proofs for many of the ideas—thereby setting mathematics on a more rigorous path than before.

Books I to VI of *Elements* deal with plane geometry—the geometry we learn in school. Books I and II deal with triangles, squares, rectangles, parallelograms, and parallels. Book I also includes the Pythagorean theorem (see pages 44–5). Book III describes the properties of circles, while Book IV deals with problems involving circles. Book V looks at commensurable and incommensurable magnitudes—mostly lines. (A commensurable magnitude being where two lengths form a ratio that is rational; while incommensurable means that the ratio is irrational.) Applications of the results from Book V are dealt with in Book VI.

Books VII to IX deal with number theory. Book VII includes the Euclidian algorithm for finding the greatest common factor of a pair of numbers. (This is covered in more detail on page 56–7.) It also discusses primes and divisibility. Book VIII looks at the geometric progression of numbers—the exercise on pages 148–9 is a geometric progression. Among other things, Book IX looks at sums of geometric series and perfect numbers (see page 17). While Book X again looks at irrational numbers—something that gave Pythagoras a real headache, and we'll revisit on pages 104–5.

Books XI through to XIII deal with three-dimensional geometry. With book XII looking at the areas and volumes of spheres, cones, cylinders, and pyramids. While Book XIII, the last book, deals with the properties of the five regular polyhedra (the Platonic solids discussed on pages 52–3) and gives a proof that there are only five such shapes. The golden ratio, which we've seen already and will meet again on pages 100–1, is also discussed.

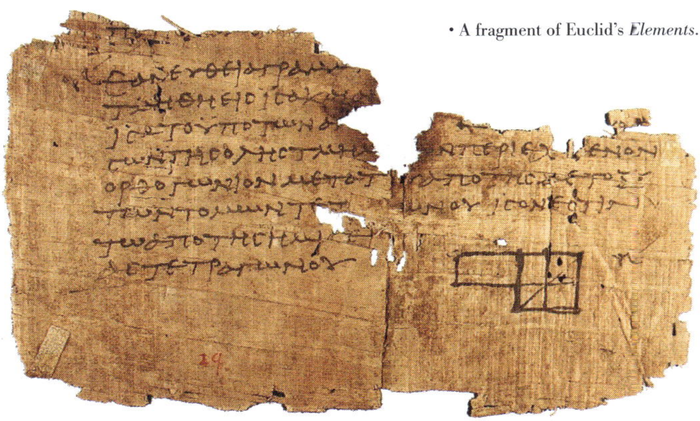

• A fragment of Euclid's *Elements*.

Exercise 8

Euclid's Algorithm

THE PROBLEM:

A town council has just started to redevelop the town square. The square has an open area measuring 602 ft by 322 ft, and the town council wants to use square concrete blocks to pave the area. They want these blocks to be as large as possible—the thought of having 193,844 tiles measuring one square foot each is out of the question. Can you find the dimensions of the largest possible square tiles that can be used so that none of the tiles needs to be cut? In other words you need a whole number of tiles in both directions—and no, there cannot be one giant tile; that's cheating!

THE METHOD:

What we need to do is find the greatest common factor of the length and width. There are a number of approaches to this. The first is to make a factor tree (see page 30) for both numbers and find what primes are common.

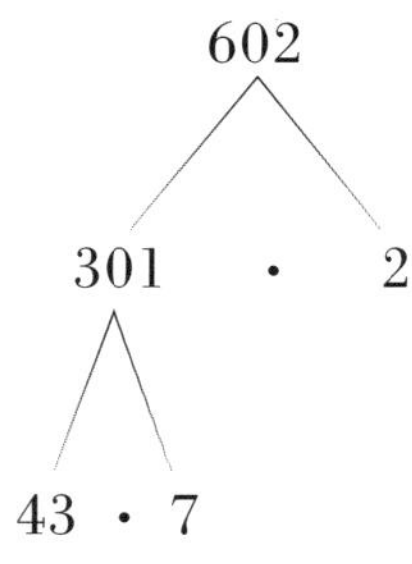

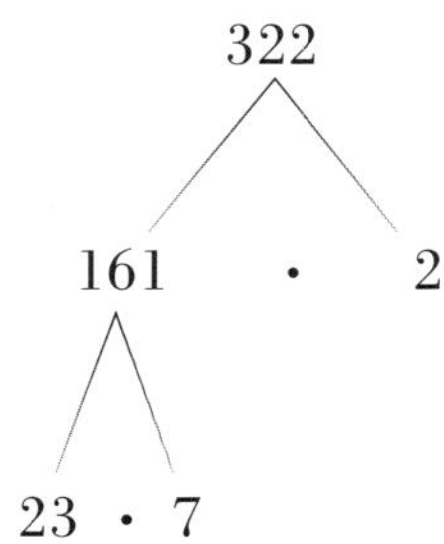

- Factor trees find all the common primes. From these primes we can find the greatest common factor.

The factors of 602 are 2, 7, and 43. That is to say that $602 = 2 \cdot 7 \cdot 43$.

The factors of 322 are 2, 7, and 23. That is to say that $322 = 2 \cdot 7 \cdot 23$.

The primes that these two numbers have in common are 2 and 7, therefore the greatest common factor is 14, or $(2 \cdot 7)$.

This method is handy, but requires that you have an affinity for primes. Let's face it, how many of us know, off the top of our heads, that 43 and 23 are primes? Also, if the dimensions of the square were slightly different, say 601 ft by 317 ft, we would be in deep trouble, because both 601 and 317 are primes. This method would have the town council using 1 ft^2 tiles.

Another method is found in Euclid's *Elements* (see pages 54–5). In Book VII, Euclid demonstrates an algorithm for finding greatest common factors that only needs you to understand long division. It works like this:

Divide the larger number by the smaller number (602 by 322):

$$\begin{array}{r} 1 \\ 322\overline{)602} \\ \underline{322} \\ 280 \end{array} \quad \textit{remainder}$$

You get 1 with a remainder of 280. Now you divide 322 by 280:

$$\begin{array}{r} 1 \\ 280\overline{)322} \\ \underline{280} \\ 42 \end{array} \quad \textit{remainder}$$

You get 1 with a remainder of 42. Now you divide 280 by 42:

$$\begin{array}{r} 6 \\ 42\overline{)280} \\ \underline{252} \\ 28 \end{array} \quad \textit{remainder}$$

You get 6 with a remainder of 28. Now you divide 42 by 28:

$$\begin{array}{r} 1 \\ 28\overline{)42} \\ \underline{28} \\ 14 \end{array} \quad \textit{remainder}$$

You get 1 with a remainder of 14. Now you divide 28 by 14:

$$\begin{array}{r} 2 \\ 14\overline{)28} \\ \underline{28} \\ 0 \end{array} \quad \textit{remainder}$$

THE SOLUTION:

You get 2 with zero remainder, so you have found your greatest common factor, 14. Therefore the council should make the concrete squares 14 ft by 14 ft.

Profile Archimedes

If Euclid is the geometry guy then Archimedes is the all-round guy. In fact, when mathematicians rate their greatest, Archimedes is up there with Newton and Gauss (see pages 144–5). However, not much is known about the personal life of Archimedes. He was born in Syracuse, on Sicily in 287 BCE, and he spent most of his life there—although there is a belief that he traveled to Alexandria and spent some time at its famous library. When in Egypt it's likely that Archimedes studied with the successors of Euclid, and in the preface of *On Spirals*, he makes reference to his friends in Alexandria, who likely included Eratosthenes (see pages 62–3).

• An ancient floor mosaic depicts the killing of Archimedes by a Roman soldier. Archimedes is said to have cried, "Do not disturb my circles."

A Eureka Moment

Though little is known for certain about the life of Archimedes, there are some great stories. One such tale, probably the most famous, deals with a crown of gold which was given as a gift to King Hiero II of Sicily (270–215 BCE), who may have been a relative of Archimedes.

Hiero wanted to know if the crown was pure gold or just an alloy. Now, Archimedes would have been able to answer the question quickly if the crown had been a cube or some other regular shape, but unfortunately it was irregular, as crowns tend to be. Knowing that different metals have different densities, that is to say different weights for the same volume, all Archimedes had to do was compare the weight of the crown to the equivalent volume of gold. But the problem that set Archimedes puzzling was: "How do I find the volume of such an irregular shape?"

Presumably the problem got him all hot and bothered, because Archimedes decided to take the most famous bath in history. As he was getting in he noticed that the water level began to rise. And, reasoning that the water level rose by a volume equivalent to that displaced by his body, Archimedes realized he had found the solution to the problem with the crown.

He was so excited that he ran out into the street yelling "Eureka, Eureka!" Or "I have found it!" We can only guess what his neighbors thought as the genius streaked past.

"Give me a place to stand and I will move the Earth."

Me and My Death Ray

Another intriguing tale concerns Archimedes' futuristic-sounding "death ray." With Syracuse threatened by Roman invasion, legend has it that Archimedes placed soldiers bearing polished copper shields around the bay in the shape of a parabola (see pages 96–7). As the fleet approached, the men focused the Sun's reflected rays onto a ship, causing it to burst into flames.

Over the years this story has been tested quite a few times, the TV show "MythBusters" being the most recent. Though it's unlikely it worked in this case, it's the same principle that used to collect TV signals. Your satellite receiver bounces the signals off the dish to collect at the receiver (the node at the end of the arm).

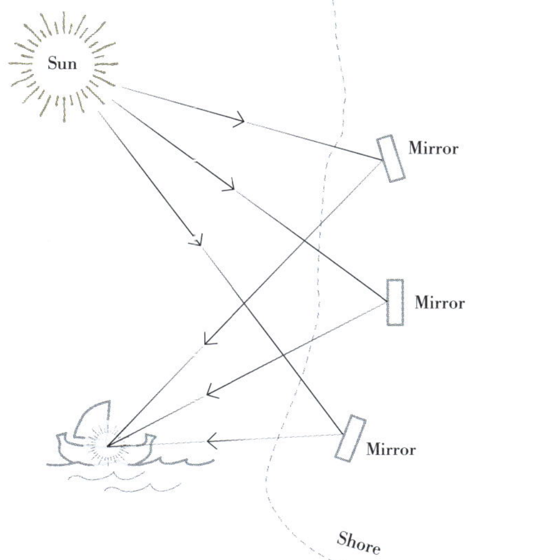

• **Archimedes' Heat Ray** Reminiscent of little boys with magnifying glasses, Archimedes' heat ray is said to have worked by focusing the power of the Sun to an intense point.

Don't Bug Me, I'm Working

This last story deals with the death of Archimedes. During the siege of Syracuse, the Roman general, Marcellus, gave strict instructions that Archimedes was not to be harmed.

Absorbed in a mathematical problem, Archimedes was unaware that the city had fallen, and when a Roman soldier happened upon him and commanded that he follow him to Marcellus, he declined. The soldier cut him down, and as he died Archimedes pleaded, "Do not disturb my circles."

Major Works

• **On the Equilibrium of Planes**
A two-volume work on centers of gravity and levers.

• **On the Measurement of a Circle**
A fraction of a longer work, which contains Archimedes' approximation of π (see pages 18–19) among other propositions.

• **On Spirals**
Contains a description of the "spiral of Archimedes."

• **On Spheres and Cylinders**
Contains the proof that the volume of an inscribed sphere is two-thirds the volume of the cylinder. A sculpted sphere and cylinder were placed on Archimedes' tomb.

• **On Floating Bodies**
Though there is no mention of his "Eureka!" moment in this work, Archimedes gives his principle of buoyancy.

• **The Sand Reckoner**
Archimedes estimates the number of grains of sand in the universe, and had to create a system for very large numbers to do so.

ARCHIMEDEAN SOLIDS

The Platonic solids that we've already met are regular, in other words all of their faces are identical, the Archimedean solids—named after Archimedes (see pages 58–9)—are called semi-regular because they have two or more face types.

Though the Archimedean solids have different faces, their vertices are regular (in other words they are all the same). These shapes look stranger, and are certainly less familiar in our everyday lives than the Platonic solids. However, looking at the number of faces, edges, and vertices, we can see the relationship the Platonic solids displayed, namely $F + V - E = 2$, also holds true for the Archimedean solids.

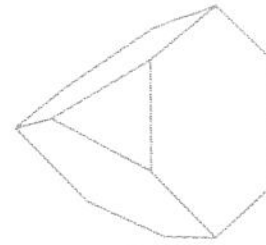

1

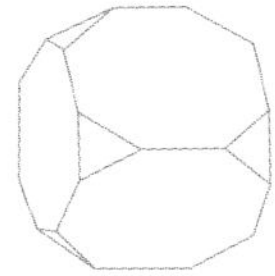

2

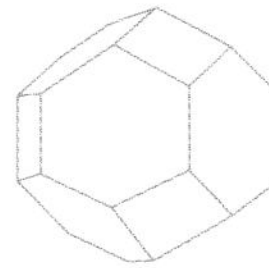

3

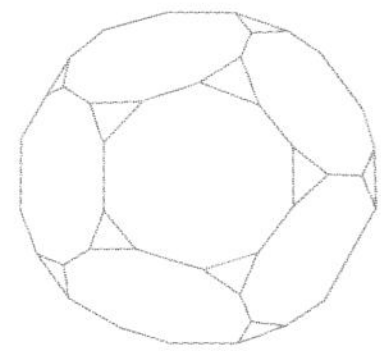

4

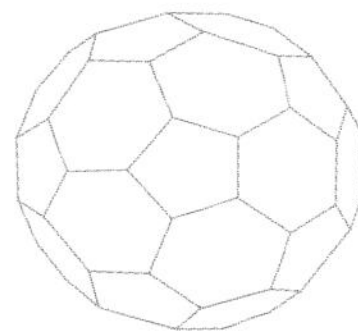

5

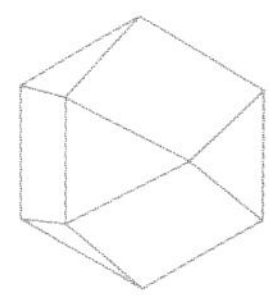

6

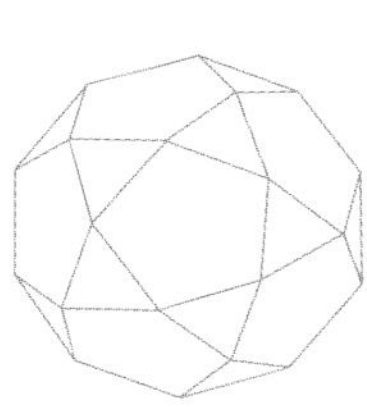

7

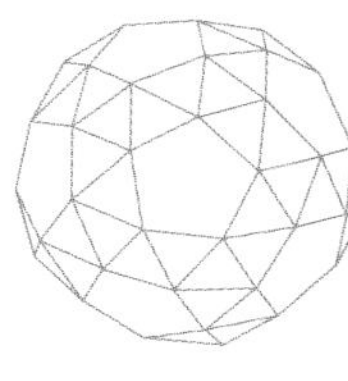

8

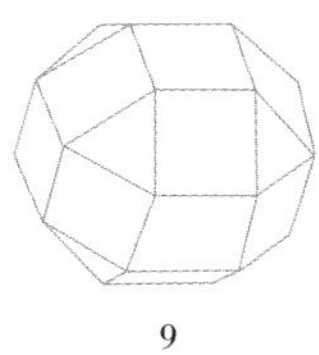

9

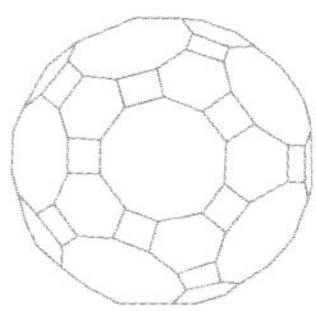

10

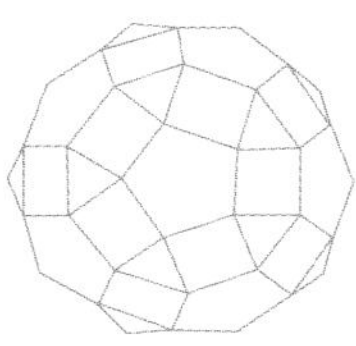

11

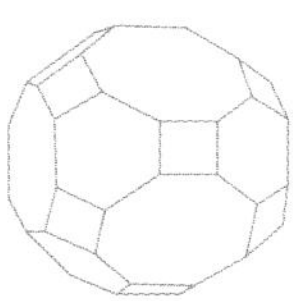

12

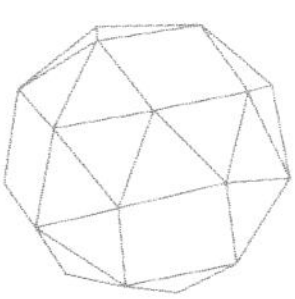

13

• The Archimedean solids might look strange, but one should be a bit more familiar. The fifth shape is essentially the form of some soccer balls—anyone for a game of truncated-icosahedron-ball?

FACE VALUE: THE ARCHIMEDEAN SOLIDS

Name	Faces	Vertices	Edges
1. Truncated tetrahedron	8 (4 triangles, 4 hexagons)	12	18
2. Truncated cube (hexahedron)	14 (8 triangles, 6 octagons)	24	36
3. Truncated octahedron	14 (6 squares, 8 hexagons)	24	36
4. Truncated dodecahedron	32 (20 triangles, 12 decagons)	60	90
5. Truncated icosahedron	32 (12 pentagons, 20 hexagons)	60	90
6. Cuboctahedron	14 (8 triangles, 6 squares)	12	24
7. Icosidodecahedron	32 (20 triangles, 12 decagons)	30	60
8. Snub dodecahedron	92 (80 triangles, 12 pentagons)	60	150
9. Small rhombicuboctahedron	26 (8 triangles, 18 squares)	24	48
10. Great rhombicosidodecahedron	62 (30 squares, 20 hexagons, 12 decagons)	120	180
11. Small rhombicosidodecahedron	62 (20 triangles, 30 squares ,12 pentagons)	60	120
12. Great rhombicuboctahedron	26 (12 squares, 8 hexagons, 6 octagons)	48	72
13. Snub cube (hexahedron)	38 (32 triangles, 6 squares)	24	60

Profile # Eratosthenes

The Moon landing was faked, there were two shooters in Dallas, and the world is flat. It's amazing that the idea of a flat Earth survived for so long in medieval Europe, when so much evidence suggests otherwise. Firstly there's the gradual disappearance of ships on the horizon. Secondly, the Sun, Moon, and to a lesser extent the stars all appear round. Lastly, during an eclipse the shadow cast is round. Given that the scientists of the ancient world had figured this out, it's weird that the idea was later lost.

Life of Eratosthenes

Eratosthenes was a Greek mathematician and astronomer born in Cyrene, which is now part of modern-day Libya, in 276 BCE. Eratosthenes has many accomplishments to his name. As an astronomer, he calculated the circumference of the Earth, the distance from the Earth to the Moon, and the distance from the Earth to the Sun. As a student he studied under Ariston of Chios, a student of Zeno. As a teacher he tutored Philopater, the son of Ptolemy III, whose grandfather was Ptolemy I, one of Alexander the Great's generals.

As a mathematician he is known for a method of determining prime numbers called "the sieve of Eratosthenes." As a geographer he made the first maps of the known world and charted the Nile. Eratosthenes also gave us a calendar with a leap year. Given these accomplishments it's perhaps a little unkind that Eratosthenes was given the nickname "beta" or "second" because he was good at so many things, but never the best. In his last years Eratosthenes went blind and it's said that in 195 BCE he committed suicide by starvation.

Around the World

Eratosthenes' calculation of the circumference of the Earth is incredible, though some doubt its validity given the many variables and errors possible. Nevertheless, it's an exceptional exercise in mathematics.

Eratosthenes noticed that at noon during the summer solstice there were no shadows in the town of Syene, now Aswan, Egypt. (Actually there would have been a small shadow because Aswan is slightly north of the Tropic of Cancer.)

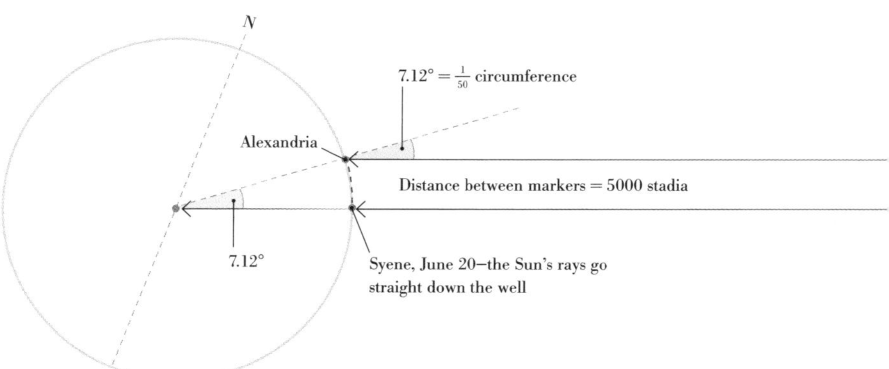

Major Works

• **PLATONICUS (LOST)**
A work that dealt with the mathematics of Plato's philosophy. Although it's now lost, we know of it via the Theon of Smyrna (c. 70–135 CE), who worked with prime and geometrical numbers as well as music.

• **ON MEANS (LOST)**
Another lost work on geometry. Mentioned by the Greek geometer Pappus (290–350 CE), who claimed it to be one of the greatest books on geometry.

• **ON THE MEASUREMENT OF THE EARTH (LOST)**
In this work, which is also lost, Eratosthenes calculated the circumference of the Earth. We know of it via the Greek astronomer Cleomedes (c. 10–70 CE) and Theon of Smyrna.

He then measured the angle of the shadow during the summer solstice in Alexandria to be 7° 12' or 7.2°—a very accurate measurement. This represented $\frac{7.2°}{360°}$ or $\frac{1}{50}$ of the circumference of the Earth. That was the easy part.

So now he knew that the distance from Syene to Alexandria is $\frac{1}{50}$ of the Earth's circumference, but how far is it from Syene to Alexandria? Eratosthenes stated that it was 5000 stadia, but how far is a stadion? Various estimates peg the value somewhere between 157 m and 185 m. The distance from Alexandria to Aswan is 843 km; dividing that by 5000 would would make a stadion 169 m, assuming the measurer moved in a direct line from one place to the other. However, this simple assumption is actually quite unlikely because Eratosthenes stated that Alexandria is to the north of Syene when in fact it's to the northwest. Also, you have to consider that traveling in a straight line without any of our modern gadgets would be pretty difficult, what with the desert and a twisting Nile in your way.

So let's accept all the possible errors—there are more besides—and calculate the upper and lower values for the Earth's circumference. If 5,000 stadia is $\frac{1}{50}$ of the circumference then 250,000 stadia would be the total circumference. At 157 m per stadion that makes the circumference of the Earth 39,250 km; at 185 m per stadion it's 46,250 km. With the true circumference at a fraction over 40,000 km, the first result is approximately a couple of percent low, while the second is 16 percent high. All in all, a remarkably accurate estimate.

• Eratosthenes' ingenious way of working out the circumference of the Earth, based on the shadows that fell on the summer solstice.

Profile

Diophantus

Diophantus is yet another enigma of the ancient world. Some mathematicians call him the "father of algebra" for his work *Arithmetica*, while others give that title to Al-Khwarizmi (see pages 86–7). Diophantus's claim to the title is based on the fact that it was in his works that the transformation from language-based mathematics to the symbol-based mathematics that we know and work with today occurred.

The Riddle of Diophantus

For a mathematician whose influences are still felt today, very little is known about Diophantus of Alexandria. Just pinning down when he lived is tough enough, and what is known about him comes mostly from secondary sources and what remains of his writing.

Diophantus lived in Alexandria during the third century. Most guess that his birth was around 200 CE and his death some eighty-four years later. This estimate come from Diophantus quoting Hypsicles (190–120 BCE), a Greek mathematician who worked with regular polyhedra (see pages 52–3 and pages 60–1), which places him some time after 150 BCE; while Theon of Alexandria (335–405 CE), another Greek mathematician and the father of Hypatia—the first known female mathematician—quotes Diophantus, which places his death before 350 CE.

His eighty-four-year lifespan comes from "The Riddle of Diophantus," which was taken from a fifth-century Greek anthology of number games. Many slightly different English versions exist, but the following is quite nice:

"Here lies Diophantus, the wonder behold

Through art Algebra, the stone tells how old:

God gave him his boyhood one-sixth of his life,

One-twelfth more as youth while whiskers grew rife;

And then yet one-seventh ere marriage begun;

In five years there came a bouncing new son.

Alas, the dear child of master and sage

After attaining half the measure his father's life chill fate took him.

After consoling his fate by the science of numbers for four years, he ended his life."

Turn to pages 66–7 for Diophantine equations.

The riddle has Diophantus living eighty-four years, but as you can imagine a word problem is not the most authoritative source. However, you take what you can get, and therein lies the uncertainty around his life. The riddle is worth solving nonetheless. If we assign x as his age at the time of his death, then the equation to find x would be:

$$x = \frac{x}{6} + \frac{x}{12} + \frac{x}{7} + 5 + \frac{x}{2} + 4$$

First we collect our xs to one side:

$$x - \frac{x}{6} - \frac{x}{12} - \frac{x}{7} - \frac{x}{2} = 9$$

Then we get a common denominator for the fractions, it's 84, and we rewrite the equation:

$$\frac{84x}{84} - \frac{14x}{84} - \frac{7x}{84} - \frac{12x}{84} - \frac{42x}{84} = 9$$

Now we subtract the numerators to get:

$$\frac{9x}{84} = 9$$

Next we multiply both sides by 84 then divide by 9 to get:

$$x = 84$$

•ARITHMETICA

Arithmetica *is a collection of problems, some say there are 130, others say 189, giving numerical solutions to determinate (a defined limit to the solution in one variable) and indeterminate equations (an infinite number of solutions in two or more variables).*

The Arithmetica *consisted of thirteen books, six of which survive. There are also four Arabic books that some think are translations of Diophantus's work. The books solve problems involving linear and quadratic equations, but Diophantus considered only positive rational solutions—in other words he ignored zero and negative numbers. (If only we could ignore the negative numbers in our bank accounts, life would be a lot easier.) The books were translated into Latin by Bombelli (see page 111) in 1570, and influence European mathematics through to the modern day. In fact, a 1621 translation by Claude Bachet, a French mathematician who wrote books on mathematical puzzles, caused Pierre de Fermat (c. 1601–65) to write in the margin "I have discovered a truly wonderful proof, but the margin is too small to contain it." It took over three hundred years for mathematicians to solve "Fermat's Last Theorem."*

•PORISMS (LOST)

In Arithmetica, *Diophantus makes reference to another work,* Porisms, *which is completely lost, although fractions of another work,* On Polygonal Numbers, *still exist.*

Exercise 9

Diophantine Equations

THE PROBLEM:

Uncle Scrooge is buying Easter eggs for his family. He has to buy for Huey, Dewey, and Louie in one house and Donald, Daisy, and Pluto in another house. Both houses must get the same number of Easter eggs and Pluto must have exactly six eggs. Find all the possible numbers of eggs the ducks will get.

THE METHOD:

The first step to solving this problem is to understand that there is not just one solution to the problem, there are many. In fact, there are an infinite number of solutions. Also, the solutions to this problem are restricted to the natural numbers (see page 14). Unless you're spectacularly mean, you're not going to give out a negative number of eggs, nor are you going to give half an egg or $\sqrt{2}$ of an egg. Equations in this form are called Diophantine equations, after Diophantus, who we've just met.

A Diophantine equation is an indeterminate equation (one with infinitely many solutions) where the variables have integer solutions only. For our example we are going back to the source. Although today integer solutions are allowed for Diophantine equations, Diophantus did not allow for zero as a solution and considered negative numbers to be absurd.

An example of a Diophantine equation is the Pythagorean theorem. This has an infinite number of (integer) solutions, so is indeterminate. Examples of solutions to the equation are: (3, 4, 5), (5, 12, 13), and multiples of these such as (6, 8, 10) and many more (see page 45 for the formula to generate Pythagorean triples).

Another type of Diophantine equation is the linear Diophantine equation in the form $ax + by = c$. An example would be $3x - 2y = 6$.

For our example we can set up an equation to solve. If we let x represent the number of eggs Huey, Dewey, and Louie each get then the number of eggs for the house will be $3x$. If we let y represent the number of eggs Donald and Daisy get, then the number of eggs for that house will be $2y + 6$ (don't forget Pluto). If the two households must equal each other then $3x = 2y + 6$ or $3x - 2y = 6$.

This is the equation of a line in standard form. To graph it we find the x- and y-intercept. To find the x-intercept we remove the y term and get $3x = 6$, therefore the x-intercept is 2. To find the y-intercept we remove the x term and get $-2y = 6$, therefore the y-intercept is -3. These represent points on the line where it crosses the x and y axes.

GRAPH 1

$(2 + 2n, 0 + 3n)$

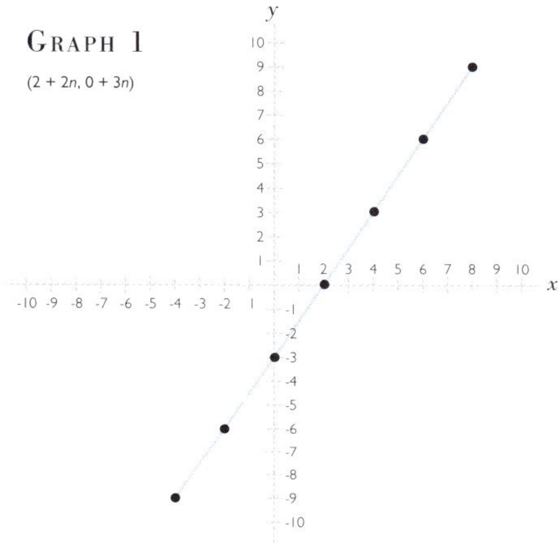

• Diophantine equations deal with integer solutions so although we can draw a line, only the points that have whole natural number solutions are allowed.

Above right is a graph of the line, and you can see that is passes through "integer solutions" (points for which there are whole numbers on the graph paper). On the graph you can see that the line passes through (2, 0) and (4, 3). The line passes through many other points—in fact, an infinite number of points—between these two points and also extends in both directions.

Diophantine equations are not interested in the rational and irrational solutions, only the integer solutions. There are also an infinite number of integer solutions; luckily once you have one of the points the others are easy to find. To move from the point (2, 0) to the point (4, 3) you must simply move up three and over two, the next Diophantine solution (to the right) will be another three up and and another two to the right at (6, 6). This pattern continues in both directions to infinity, and beyond... Since we cannot write an infinite number of solutions we write $(2 + 2n, 0 + 3n)$, where n is an integer. Therefore, when $n = 1$ we have (4, 3); when $n = 2$ we have (6, 6); when $n = 3$ we get (8, 9), and so on.

THE SOLUTION:

Huey, Dewey, and Louie will get $2 + 2n$ eggs, while Donald and Daisy will get $0 + 3n$ eggs, and Pluto will get 6 eggs. (Note that n is a natural number.)

Chapter

3

Egypt, India, and Persia

As we mentioned at the start of the previous chapter, our keen awareness of the ancient Greeks perhaps blinds us to the mathematical advances made elsewhere. However, the fact is that key figures such as Brahmagupta, Al-Khwarizmi, and Omar Khayyam, alongside many other Eastern mathematicians, made contributions to our modern understanding of maths that were arguably even more profound than those of the ancient Greeks.

EGYPTIAN MATHEMATICS

Ancient Egyptian mathematics was really quite advanced. Like us, the ancient Egyptians had a base-ten system, but unlike ours it wasn't a place-value system. Instead they had separate symbols to represent the one, ten, a hundred, a thousand, ten thousand, and a million. I love the kneeling guy for a million; I can just picture some ancient Egyptian on his knees shouting: "Yes, I've won a million… I'm rich!"

Ancient Egyptian Arithmetic

The Egyptian hieroglyphs used to represent numbers are shown below; and it's easy to use these to represent other numbers. For example, one is represented by the figure I so any number up to nine can be represented by that many Is; for instance, three would be III.

You can also make larger numbers quite simply. When you reach the next hieroglyph up, you simply use that at the beginning; for example, 123 would be written as ϱ∩∩III.

Adding and subtracting is also easy, and uses a system of carrying forward and borrowing, much like we do today. As an example, let's add two numbers: twenty-eight and 103; or in Egyptian numerals ∩∩IIIIIIII (28) and ϱIII (103).

We just add the units together to get eleven, which is a one and a ten. That is to say IIIIIIIIIII = ∩I, which is like the carrying forward we do in our base-ten arithmetic. Then we do the same for the tens and the hundreds. So:

28 + 103 = 131 or ∩∩IIIIIIII + ϱIII = ϱ∩∩∩I

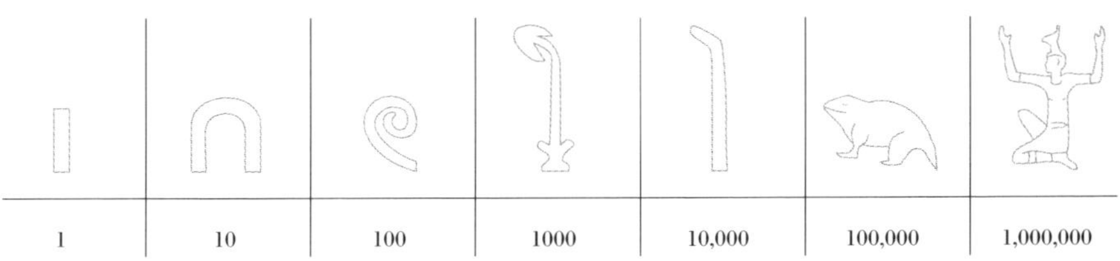

• Egyptian numeral hieroglyphics It's interesting that the Egyptians used a base-ten number system, while later the Greeks and Romans did not. The Greeks and Romans included symbols for other values such as five, fifty, and so on. The base-ten system would only reappear from the East many centuries later.

Multiplication and division are a little more complicated, but the method used is quite interesting. What the Egyptians did was to successively double one of the two numbers. Let's try 11 • 26.

∩∩|||||| = one 26
∩∩∩∩∩|| = two 26s
𓍢|||| = four 26s
𓍢𓍢|||||||| = eight 26s

Now to make eleven 26s they would just add the eight, two, and one 26s that we worked out above. We have a total of sixteen units so we carry the ten to the next symbol and leave six units. We now have a total of eight tens, and two hundreds, which can be written as:

𓍢𓍢∩∩∩∩∩∩∩∩|||||| = 286

Ancient Egyptian Fractions

The ancient Egyptians also had a method for dealing with fractions. To write a fraction they would just add an "eye" symbol above the number that represented the divisor; so $\frac{1}{2}$ would look like $\overset{\frown}{||}$ and $\frac{1}{10}$ would be $\overset{\frown}{\cap}$.

This limited the Egyptians to using only unit fractions—those fractions where the numerator (the top number) is always one. But to make other fractions they would just add unit fractions together; for example, $\frac{5}{6}$ would be $\frac{1}{2} + \frac{1}{3}$ or $\overset{\frown}{||} + \overset{\frown}{|||}$.

Some people suggest that the use of unit fractions in Greece can be traced back to the ancient Egyptians.

THE RHIND AND MOSCOW PAPYRI

The Rhind Papyrus is named after the Scottish Egyptologist, A. Henry Rhind who purchased the papyrus in Egypt in 1858. It's a scroll about 20 ft (6 m) long and 1 ft (30 cm) wide. It was written around 1650 BCE by Ahmes, a scribe who states that he was copying an earlier text that was a couple of hundred years older still. Therefore the material on the papyrus possibly dates from as long ago as 1850 BCE.

Some eighty-seven problems are contained on the papyrus, ranging from those dealing with basic arithmetic—though with Egyptian numerals, division and multiplication were not that easy—to geometry and equation solving. Though the papyrus deals with problems that would involve equations, they are not like those we know—the beginnings of algebra as we understand it would not appear for centuries.

The Moscow Papyrus, or the Golenishchev Papyrus, is roughly 15 ft (4.5 m) and 3 in (7 cm) wide. It consists of twenty-five problems that are mostly geometric in nature.

The Moscow Papyrus is now held at the Museum of Fine Arts in Moscow and the Rhind Papyrus is at the British Museum in London.

Exercise

10 Completing the Square

THE PROBLEM:

Quadratic equations (where x^2 is the leading term) have many real-life applications, and here we'll look at their role in gravity, albeit crudely. In our first problem, Noel and Liam are having a balloon fight over a fence. Noel fires a balloon and it follows a parabola (see pages 96–7), which can be represented by $h = -x^2 - 6x + 40$. Where h is the height and x is the distance (in meters) to the left and right of the fence. How far behind the fence was Noel when he shot the balloon and how far over the fence did it land?

THE METHOD

There are many ways to solve quadratic equations. Completing the square is one technique, and first we're going to look at it from a geometric point of view. The first thing we should note is that we're trying to find out when the balloon hits the ground. The ground represents a height of zero, therefore $h = 0$. The equation will now be:

$$0 = -x^2 - 6x + 40$$

For simplicity, we will add x^2 and $6x$ to both sides to get the equation:

$$x^2 + 6x = 40$$

This helps us because the positive numbers allow a geometric solution. Now x^2 can represent a square with sides that are both of the length x, and $6x$ can

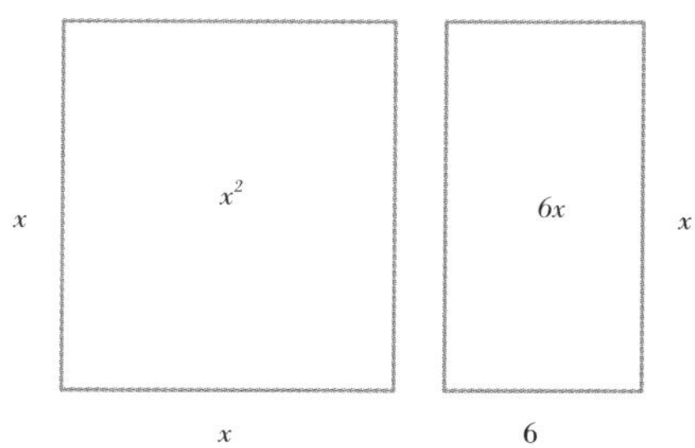

represent a rectangle with one side that is x long and one that is 6 long.

Adding these two shapes, as the left-hand side of the equation ($x^2 + 6x$ ...) indicates, makes a rectangle that measures x on one side and $x + 6$ on the other, in other words $x \cdot (x + 6)$. At this point we could guess what x is, and if the number happens to be an integer we might get lucky. But if the answer is rational or irrational then things get trickier.

We're "completing the square," not a rectangle, so we need to divide the $6x$ rectangle into two equal rectangles, both measuring $3x$, and place them on either side of the square.

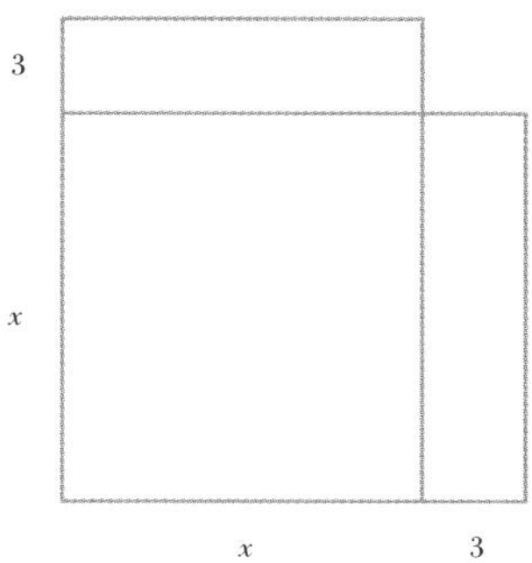

Now we complete the square by filling in the top right corner. The little square measures 3 by 3, so we perform the simple multiplication to find that we need to add 9—remember to add it to both sides. This gives:

$$(x + 3)^2 = 49$$

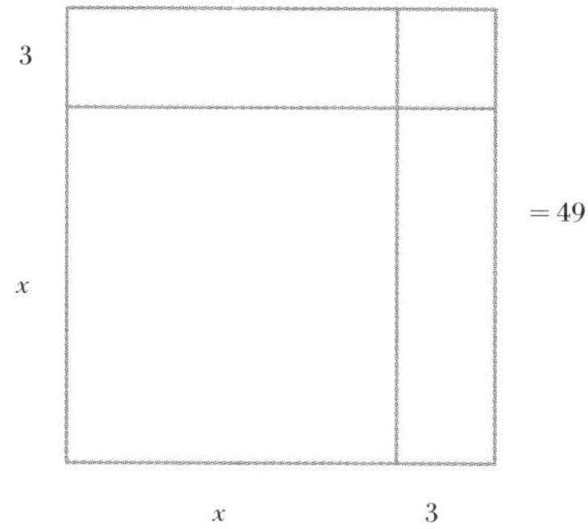

We now have to ask ourselves, what number, when squared, is equal to 49? Well, 7^2 is 49, therefore $x + 3$ must equal 7 and that would mean $x = 4$.

This makes a lot of sense, but there is another value of x that is not at all obvious from this geometric approach. Diophantus (see pages 64–5) called negative answers absurd, but in theoretical mathematics they are answers nonetheless. These must be considered when solving the problem. In this case, $(-7)^2$ also equals 49, therefore $x + 3$ must equal -7 as well, and that would make $x = -10$. Let's face it, it's pretty hard to draw a square that measures -10, thus the aversion to negative numbers when you view the problem from a geometric stance.

THE SOLUTION:

Taking these values of -10 and 4 means Noel was 10 meters to the left of the fence when he shot the balloon and it landed 4 meters to the right of the fence. (Whether it hit Liam is open to debate.)

INDIAN MATHEMATICS

Everybody uses numbers in their everyday lives, but most of us do so without a thought for where they're from. We're far more familiar with the etymology of words and the development of our language; but numbers play a crucial role in our lives, so why are so few people inspired to ask: "Where do our numbers come from?"

The Indian Sulbasutras

Sulbasutras are appendices to religious texts. They were not theoretical texts, but rather applied mathematics to do with the construction of religious architecture.

In the sulbasutra of Baudhayana (c. 800–740 BCE) the Pythagorean theorem—or at least a special case of it, the right-angled isosceles triangle—is dealt with. Again, our reference to Pythagoras, given that he would not be born for another two hundred years, reveals our Eurocentric view of the mathematical world. In the sulbasutra of Katyayana (c. 200–140 BCE) there is reference to the theorem without restrictions, though this was after the time of Pythagoras.

Somewhat earlier, two sulbasutras, that of Apastamba, who lived in the sixth century BCE, and Katyayana (third century BCE), gave a value for the square root of two (see page 32) of $\frac{577}{408}$, which is accurate to the fifth decimal place.

Given that these texts deal with construction, circles come into play. Interestingly, the approximations for the value of π change depending on the nature of the calculation. It seems the applied nature of the sulbasutras made an exact value unnecessary. Values used for π ranged from about 3 to 3.2.

The Indian Numerals

The true significance of the Indian contribution was commented upon by the French mathematician Pierre-Simon Laplace (1749–1827):

"It is India that gave us the ingenious method of expressing all numbers by means of ten symbols, each symbol receiving a value of position as well as an absolute value; a profound and important idea which appears so simple to us now that we ignore its true merit. But its very simplicity and the great ease which it has lent to computations put our arithmetic in the first rank of useful inventions; and we shall appreciate the grandeur of the achievement the more when we remember that it escaped the genius of Archimedes and Apollonius, two of the greatest men produced by antiquity." (Quoted in H. Eves, *Return to Mathematical Circles*; 1988.)

Laplace is right; imagine if we still tried to work with Roman numerals.

The advancements we have made would certainly have been delayed. We just have to review the difficulty in multiplying Egyptian numbers, which were at least part of a base-ten system, Roman numerals would have been worse.

Brahmi numerals, which came into use around 250 BCE, were part of a kind of base-ten system. It had distinct symbols for the first nine numbers and separate symbols for multiples of ten and one hundred. That is to say there was a symbol for twenty, thirty, four hundred, five hundred, and so on. In the seventh century CE, around the time of Brahmagupta (see pages 78–9), a base-ten positional system came into use. It's interesting that the Egyptians had a base-ten system, but not a place-value one while the Babylonians had a positional system that was base-sixty rather than ten.

Indian Mathematics

Above we discussed the sulbasutras, which contained a significant amount of mathematical knowledge, but, like the Egyptians, were focused only on its application. We now jump forward to 476 CE and the birth of Aryabhata.

Aryabhata wrote the *Aryabhatiya*, which collected all the mathematics in India up to that point—very much like Euclid collecting the rules of geometry (see pages 54–5). The *Aryabhatiya* contains arithmetic, algebra, trigonometry, and quadratic equations, and also a very accurate value for π (3.1416). The difference, though, was that Euclid provided rigorous proofs for the rules.

Then, in the sixth century, Varahamihira summarized astronomical works as well as looking at Pascal's triangle (see pages 130–5) and magic squares (see box below).

Next came Brahmagupta (see pages 78–9) who lived in the seventh century, and whose work was extended by Mahavira in the ninth century. A generation on, and Prthudakasvami continued the work on the algebra of quadratic equations; while Sridhara (870–930 CE) was one of the first to produce a general formula for solving quadratics (see pages 88–9), though for only one root.

There continued to be advances in Indian mathematics, though by the thirteenth century. and Fibonacci's introduction of Arabic numerals to Europe, the shift westward had begun.

MAGIC SQUARE

A magic square is a square where the rows, columns, and diagonals all add to the same amount. In the case shown here that is fifteen.

8	1	6
3	5	7
4	9	2

Exercise

11 Completing the Square, Revisited

THE PROBLEM:

Mick and Keith are having a balloon fight. Between them is a large fence over which they have to shoot their balloons. Mick fires a balloon over the fence and it follows the path of a parabola. The equation of the parabola is $h = -x^2 - 6x + 40$. Where h is the height above the ground and x is the distance (in meters) to the left and right of the fence. How far behind the fence was Mick when he shot the balloon and how far over the fence did it land. We're assuming that fence is the zero point.

THE METHOD

This problem may well seem familiar. However, there are many ways to solve quadratic equations, and the best way to demonstrate different methods is to use the same example, and hope that we arrive at the same solution. Here we're going to look at completing the square from an algebraic point of view.

The first thing we should note is that we're trying to find out when the balloon hits the ground. The ground represents a height of zero, therefore $h = 0$. The equation will now be $0 = -x^2 - 6x + 40$. For simplicity, we will add x^2 and $6x$ to both sides to get the equation:

$$x^2 + 6x = 40$$

Completing the square using algebra is similar to using the geometric technique on pages 72–3, just without the pictures.

First, we halve the linear term's coefficient (namely 6) which gives us 3. To compare this with the geometric approach on pages 72–3, this is like breaking the $6x$ rectangle into two.

Then we square the number 3 to get 9, and add this to both sides, giving:

$$x^2 + 6x + 9 = 40 + 9$$

Next, the left side factors into $(x + 3)(x + 3)$ or $(x + 3)^2$ to give us:

$$(x + 3)^2 = 49$$

Now we find the square root of both sides to get:

$$\sqrt{(x + 3)^2} = \pm\sqrt{49}$$

We have a plus/minus sign in front of the $\sqrt{49}$ because both 7^2 and $(-7)^2$ are equal to 49. Now a square root of a square is itself so the square root and the square simply cancel out and we get $(x + 3)$ on the left of the equation and the square root of 49 becomes ± 7 to give:

$$(x + 3) = \pm 7$$

We subtract 3 from both sides to give:

$$x = \pm 7 - 3$$

Then we work out both the negative and positive solutions:

$$x = -7 - 3 = -10$$
$$x = +7 - 3 = 4$$

THE SOLUTION:

So Mick was 10 meters to the left of the fence (a negative number) when he shot the balloon and it landed 4 meters to the right of the fence (a positive number).

GRAPH 2

$(h = -x^2 - 6x + 40)$

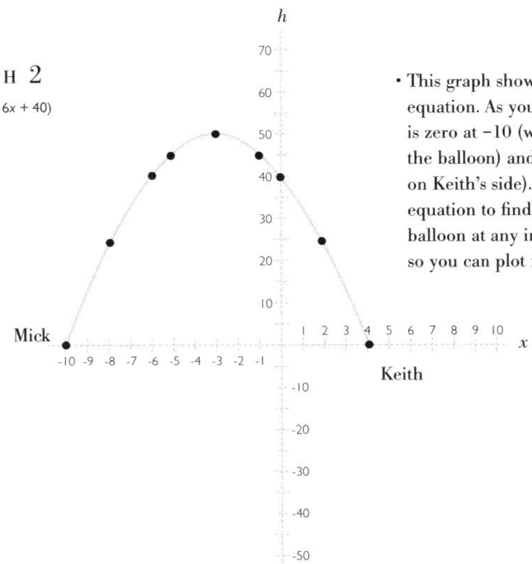

• This graph shows the parabola of the equation. As you can see, the height is zero at −10 (where Mick throws the balloon) and 4 (where it lands on Keith's side). You can also use the equation to find the height of the balloon at any intermediate distance, so you can plot its flight.

Profile

Brahmagupta

Sometimes the littlest things are the most important and simultaneously the most overlooked. For most people, this little thing is so small it's nothing, quite literally zero. It was Brahmagupta who gave us a new way of looking at zero. Mathematics up to this time had been hampered by numeral systems that would have made the calculations we do today far more difficult. The ancient Egyptians had a base-ten system, and the Babylonians had a place-value system, but it was Indians who gave us the base-ten place-value system we know today. Moreover, Brahmagupta was also the first to investigate zero as a number, not just a place holder.

Brahmagupta was born in 598 CE in the city of Bhinmal in the northwest of India near modern-day Pakistan. He was made head of the observatory in Ujjain, a city east of Bhinmal and a center of astronomy and mathematics. During his time in Ujjain, Brahmagupta wrote several texts. The *Brahmasphutasiddhanta* is the most famous of his works and is discussed below. He also produced the *Cadamekela*, *Khanda-khadyak*, and *Durkeamynarda* but very little information can be found on these works today. He died in 670 CE.

The Brahmasphutasiddhanta

In 628, at thirty years of age, Brahmagupta wrote the *Brahmasphutasiddhanta*—now that's a tongue twister—a text which has had a profound affect on Western mathematics. The *Brahmasphutasiddhanta* is divided into twenty-five chapters. The first ten are thought to be an earlier work of Brahmagupta's, while

BRAHMAGUPTA'S LAWS

The significance of Brahmagupta's laws is that they treat zero as a number, not just a place holder, and negative numbers are treated as numbers, not numerical outcasts to be ignored.

1) A zero added to a number is the number.
2) A zero subtracted from a number is the number.
3) A number times zero is zero.
4) A negative minus zero is a negative.
5) A positive minus zero is a positive.
6) Zero minus zero is zero.
7) A negative subtracted from zero is a positive.
8) A positive subtracted from zero is a negative.
9) The product of zero multiplied by a negative or positive is zero.
10) The product of zero multiplied by zero is zero.
11) The product or quotient of two positives is one positive.
12) The product or quotient of two negatives is one positive.
13) The product or quotient of a negative and a positive is a negative.
14) The product or quotient of a positive and a negative is a negative.

the next fifteen are improvements or addendums to the first ten. In the *Brahmasphutasiddhanta* several different topics are covered. Diophantine analysis (see pages 66–7) is covered in chapter twelve where Brahmagupta looks at Pythagorean triples (see page 45) and a family of equations now known as Pell's equations (see box). Brahmagupta also developed an equation for the area of a neat mathematical curiosity, the "cyclic quadrilateral" (a four-sided shape where each point touches the inside of a circle—see below).

However, by far the most important section of the *Brahmasphutasiddhanta* deals with zero and negative numbers, this covers the rules that we learn for integers around the age of twelve (see box left).

The *Brahmasphutasiddhanta* treated zero and negative numbers as potential solutions. Previously, with a geometric approach, zero and negatives had been ignored or considered absurd because in the real world zero or negative lengths or areas simply don't exist. However, as we know today, these numbers have many practical applications—I might not be able to hold a negative dollar in my hand, but I can certainly see them in my bank account.

PELL'S EQUATIONS

Pell's equations are in the form $x^2 - ny^2 = 1$. They are named after John Pell an English mathematician (1611–85) who really had little to do with their development. Brahmagupta was the first to truly study Pell's equations, but similar work has been done by Diophantus (see pages 64–5).

What makes these equations interesting is that the integer solutions approximate the root of n. That is to say the solutions to $x^2 - 2y^2 = (1)$ (3, 2), (17, 12), (577, 408) and so on, are better and better approximations for the square root of two. Note:

$$\frac{3}{2} = 1.5$$

$$\frac{17}{12} = 1.41\dot{6}$$

$$\frac{577}{408} = 1.414215686$$

where $\sqrt{2} = 1.414213563$

Brahmagupta hit a few snags along the way, especially when it came to dividing by zero. But this gives most people headaches; just ask anyone who uses calculus, whether in science, engineering, business, or medicine.

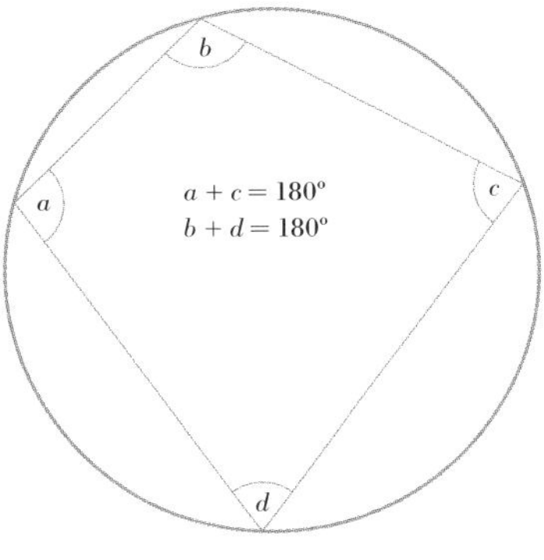

• *A cyclic quadrilateral is a four-sided shape where the vertices (corners) all touch a circle. They have neat properties, including that their opposite internal angles add to 180°.*

Exercise 12

Solving Quadratics by Decomposition

THE PROBLEM:

John and Paul have dug a shared parabolic swimming pool across their backyards. The equation of the swimming pool is $6x^2 + 5x - 21 = d$, where d is the distance below the ground and x is the number of meters on either side of the property line. How far does the pool extend into each property?

THE METHOD

The first step is to figure out exactly what we need to find. This is often the most difficult part. The pool is dug into the ground, so to find out how far it extends into each yard we need to find out the x values when the depth d is zero or solve the equation:

$$6x^2 + 5x - 21 = 0$$

One approach is to guess, picking values for x then solving the equation to see if you get zero. This is pretty impractical. You can't isolate the variable because there is an x and x^2 in the equation. There are several approaches to solving this problem.

As we saw on pages 34–5, multiplying two binomials can give us a quadratic. So the approach we're going to take now is to head in the other direction, breaking the quadratic into two binomials. Then we have to find the value of x that makes each binomial equal to zero.

Just to recap, a binomial takes the form of $(ax + b)(cx + d) = 0$, where a, b, c, and d are numbers. (See pages 32–5 if you want to brush up on binomials.)

In order to find the values of the numbers, we could guess what a, b, c, and d are, but you'll need either a little luck, or quite a lot of time to find the right answers, and if the solutions are fractions or irrational numbers guessing is more or less worthless.

Another option is to use factoring. Factoring is the opposite of "foiling." With "foiling" you multiply two binomials to create a trinomial, factoring takes the trinomial and recreates the two binomials. Factoring is fine when the solutions are rational numbers, but not so great when they're irrational. One method will be presented here, and two more on pages 84–5.

Decomposition

Step 1. Multiply the first and last numbers of the left-hand side:

$$6x^2 + 5x - 21$$

$$\searrow \quad \swarrow$$

$$-126$$

Step 2. Find a number pair that multiplies to −126 and adds to 5:

$$-126$$

$$\swarrow \quad \searrow$$

$$14 \quad -9$$

Step 3. Decompose (or break up) the middle term into that pair:

$$6x^2 + 14x - 9x - 21$$

Step 4. Find the common factors in the first and last pairs of terms: $6x^2$ and $14x$ can both be divided by 2 and x; and $-9x$ and -21 can both be divided by -3. These common factors are moved in front of the brackets containing what is left, in other words $3x + 7$ in both cases:

$$2x(3x + 7) - 3(3x + 7)$$

Step 5. Now factor out the common bracket by grouping the two terms preceding them into a single bracket to give:

$$(2x - 3)(3x + 7)$$

Solving the Binomials

Phew! Now we've factored the trinomial into two binomials it's time to make our equation equal to zero again, so we can solve the problem of how far the pool extends into each property:

$$(3x + 7)(2x - 3) = 0$$

Now, for the left side to be zero (which it has to be because the equals sign means the equation must balance) either the first or second binomial must be equal to zero. So now we need to find the values of x which make each binomial equal to zero.

$$3x + 7 = 0 \qquad 2x - 3 = 0$$

$$3x = -7 \qquad 2x = 3$$

$$x = \frac{-7}{3} \qquad x = \frac{3}{2}$$

THE SOLUTION

The solution is $x = \frac{3}{2}$ and $x = \frac{-7}{3}$ so the pool extends $\frac{7}{3}$ of a meter (2.33 m) into Paul's yard (I'm assuming his house was to the left or negative side of the number line) and $\frac{3}{2}$ of a meter (1.5 m) into John's yard.

ARABIC ALGEBRA

I remember learning about the Egyptians, Greeks, and Romans one year in school. Then at the start of the next year there was a cursory mention of the "Dark Ages," before boom ... we were in the middle of the Renaissance. It was like we went from the fall of the Western Roman Empire (in the late fifth century CE) to the dawning of the Renaissance almost a millennium later, with nothing in between. As it turns out, there was quite a lot going on, during this time the center of learning shifted east to Baghdad.

The House of Wisdom

The closing of Plato's academy in 529 CE could be considered Greek mathematics' last gasp. From that point until the thirteenth century the mathematical center of the world was in the East.

The House of Wisdom in Baghdad was established by Harun Al-Rashid (763 to 809), the fifth Caliph of the Abbasid dynasty, and his son Al-Ma'mun. Harun Al-Rashid reigned from 786 to 809, while Al-Ma'mun ruled from 813 to 833. During this time the Islamic empire stretched from Spain in the west to the borders of India in the east. It's this connection to India that will become important.

Originally the House of Wisdom was focused on translating and preserving works from Persia, then Greece, and India. Over time it became a center for studies in humanities and sciences, until it was destroyed during the Mongol invasion of 1258.

Though little is said about Persian mathematicians, there have been many of significance. Starting around the time of the founding of the House of Wisdom, we have Al-Khwarizmi (see pages 86–7). Then Al-Kindi, who lived from 801 to 873, and wrote on Indian number systems. Around the same time, the three Banu Musa brothers worked on geometry, astronomy, and mechanics.

Abu Kamil, who was born in 850 and died in 930, extended Al-Khwarizmi's work on algebra. Then Ibrahim ibn Sinan, who was born in 908 and lived for only thirty-eight years, extended the theory of integration, taking Archimedes' method of exhaustion further. Finally, Al-Karaji (953–1029) made significant advances in algebra, making it much more like what we know today and less like geometry.

There are a host of other mathematicians who either translated texts, made commentaries on text, or furthered mathematics in the areas of geometry, trigonometry, number theory, and so on.

Arabic Numerals

One of the most significant advances made during this time was the adoption of a base-ten place-value system for numbers. In other words, a system that has ten symbols, and within which the place of the symbol determines its value.

Sound familiar? Well, the system we work with today is a base-ten place-value system. That is to say when we write the number 535, we know the numerals have different values based on their position, so the first five relates to "hundreds" and the last five to "units."

As we've already seen, the ancient Egyptians had a base-ten system, but not a place-value one—they had a different symbol for each power of ten. This made things like multiplication very difficult (see pages 70–1). Roman numerals were even more difficult to deal with.

The base-ten place-value system allows for easier methods of calculation and the development of decimals. This matters because making arithmetic simpler frees up mathematicians to think about the bigger picture—consider how much easier the number-crunching power of computers makes it for today's scientists to think profound thoughts.

Arabic numerals began their life as Indian numerals. A Christian bishop living near the Euphrates River wrote of their use in 662, but the earliest surviving text that contains them is from the tenth century. A twelfth-century Latin text *Algoritmi de Numero Indorum*, (a translation of an Al-Khwarizmi text), is often claimed to be the first Arabic text on Indian numerals. This dates the adoption of Indian numerals to between 790 and 840. It's interesting to note that our word "algorithm" comes from the title of this text. In 1202 Fibonacci introduced Arabic numerals to Europe.

• The development of Indian–Arabic numerals into something approaching the numbers we use in everyday life.

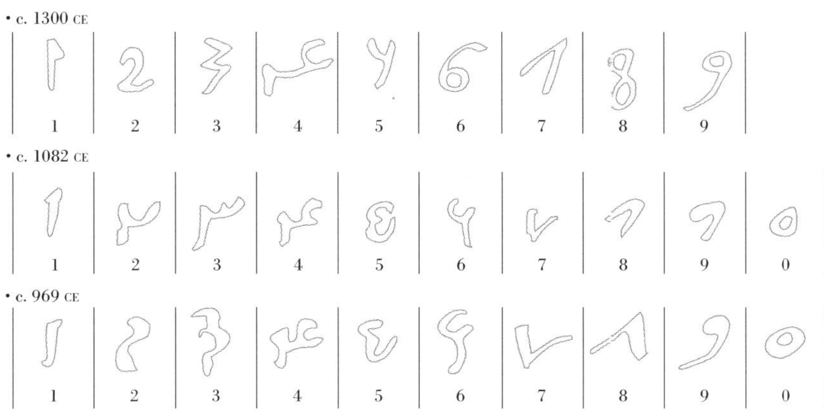

Exercise 13

Down Under and BaRF

THE PROBLEM:

George and Ringo have dug a shared parabolic swimming pool in their backyards. The equation of the swimming pool is $6x^2 + 5x - 21 = d$, where d is the distance below the ground and x is the number of meters away from the property line. How far does the pool extend into each property?

THE METHOD

I know this problem might give you a sense of déjà-vu, but it's really entirely different from the one on pages 80–1. See how I've changed the names to George and Ringo? It gives a completely different flavor to the question.

Yes, of course the problem is the same. However, quadratic equations and parabolas (the graphs that quadratic equations make) are important, and can be found, for example, in the calculation of certain rare orbits, the cables of a suspended-deck bridge, and even the reflector of a flashlight.

Solving quadratic equations can be done in many ways. As I explained a little earlier, the best way to demonstrate multiple techniques is to use the same example, and we'll try a few different methods here.

Down Under

Step 1. Multiply the first and last numbers of the left-hand side:

$$6x^2 + 5x - 21 = d$$

↘ ↙

$$-126$$

Step 2. Find a number pair that multiplies to −126 and adds to the middle number, which is 5:

$$-126$$

↙ ↘

$$14 \quad -9$$

Step 3. Write two binomials using the coefficient (in this case 6) for the leading terms and the denominator, and the number pair for the trailing terms:

$$\frac{(6x + 14)(6x - 9)}{6}$$

Step 4. Take the common factors out of the binomials. A 2 is common in the first bracket and a 3 in the second, the denominator is common to both:

$$\left(\frac{2 \cdot 3}{6}\right)(3x + 7)(2x - 3)$$

Step 5. Solve the first brackets to give:

$$(3x + 7)(2x - 3)$$

BaRF (Brackets, a, Reduce, Fly)

Step 1. Multiply the first and last numbers on the left-hand side:

$$6x^2 + 5x - 21 = d$$

$$\searrow \quad \swarrow$$

$$-126$$

Step 2. Find a number pair that multiplies to −126 and adds to the middle number, which is 5:

$$-126$$

$$\swarrow \quad \searrow$$

$$14 \quad -9$$

Step 3 (Brackets). Write the binomials using that number pair; ignore the coefficient 6 for the time being:

$$(x + 14)(x - 9)$$

Step 4 (a). Add the *a* term (see page 80, in this case it's the x^2 coefficient, which is 6) in the denominator:

$$\left(x + \frac{14}{6}\right)\left(x - \frac{9}{6}\right)$$

Step 5 (Reduce). Simplify your fractions:

$$\left(x + \frac{7}{3}\right)\left(x - \frac{3}{2}\right)$$

Step 6 (Fly). Move the denominator to the front of each binomial:

$$(3x + 7)(2x - 3)$$

Solving the Binomials

Now we've tried a couple of methods for factoring the trinomial into two binomials we need to solve them. So we make the equation equal to zero again.

$$(3x + 7)(2x - 3) = 0$$

Now, for the left side to be zero, either the first or second binomial must equal zero. Next we find the values of *x* which make each binomial equal to zero.

$$3x + 7 = 0 \qquad 2x - 3 = 0$$

$$3x = -7 \qquad 2x = 3$$

$$x = \frac{-7}{3} \qquad x = \frac{3}{2}$$

THE SOLUTION

The solution is $x = \frac{3}{2}$ and $x = \frac{-7}{3}$ so the pool extends $\frac{7}{3}$ of a meter (2.33 m) into George's yard (I am assuming his house was to the left or negative side of the number line) and $\frac{3}{2}$ of a meter (1.5 m) in Ringo's yard.

Profile # Al-Khwarizmi

Much like Euclid, the Greek "father of geometry" and the author of one of the greatest books of all time, *Elements*, very little is known about Al-Khwarizmi. Most people will find this amazing, as they've never heard of him, but it's from Al-Khwarizmi that we get two household words—at least they are if you live in my house—algebra and algorithm.

Al-Khwarizmi, or Abu Ja'far Muhammad ibn Musa Al-Khwarizmi, was born around 780 CE, although exactly where he was born is a subject of some debate. Some think that he came from Khwarezm, which is now in Uzbekistan, south of the Aral Sea and east of the Caspian, while others suggest he was born in Baghdad.

One thing that is known for sure is that Al-Khwarizmi worked at the House of Wisdom (see pages 82–3). When there, Al-Khwarizmi worked with the Banu Musa brothers as translators of Greek, Indian, and other texts. He also expanded on these translations by writing his own texts on algebra, geometry, astronomy, and geography.

• **Al-Khwarizmi** Anyone studying mathematics or its history should know the name Al-Khwarizmi, one of the key figures in the development of algebra.

Al-Khwarizmi completed several texts of consequence. One major work was *Kitab Surat Al-Ard*, written in 833. It revised Ptolemy's *Geography*, including the coordinates of over 2,400 cities and geographical features. In *Kitab Surat Al-Ard*, Al-Khwarizmi corrected Ptolemy's overestimation of the length of the Mediterranean Sea and added details about lands to the east, which were better known to the Abbasid dynasty than to the Greeks. Al-Khwarizmi also wrote several minor works on astrolabes (an instrument used by astronomers, astrologers, and navigators), sundials, and the Jewish calendar. However, his two biggest works are coming right up.

The Origins of "Algorithm"

Al-Khwarizmi's second most important work was *Algoritmi de Numero Indorum*, the title of a Latin translation of his original Arabic text, which has been lost.

It's from this title that we get the word algorithm, which means a number of steps or instructions to be followed. In this work Al-Khwarizmi introduces the Hindu place-value system for numerals. It's also believed that this is the first use of zero as a place holder. For most of my life I didn't really care, or just assumed that the numbers we used were European; then I thought that they were Arabic, and only later did I learn that they came from further east, namely India. It's interesting just how wrong our assumptions about the world can be.

In the text, Al-Khwarizmi gives methods for calculations and also a method for finding square roots.

The Origins of "Algebra"

Hisab Al-Jabr w'Al-Muqabala, is the most significant work that was produced by Al-Khwarizmi, and it's from the "Al-Jabr" part of the title that we get the word algebra. Though some scholars consider Diophantus (see pages 64–5) to be the "father of algebra," others believe that title belongs to Al-Khwarizmi because of his work in this text.

Al-Khwarizmi's method for solving linear and quadratic equations was to reduce the equations to one of six forms. This meant that Al-Khwarizmi could neatly sidestep the problems that were posed by negative numbers. At this point it's interesting to define the parts of a quadratic according to Al-Khwarizmi. Given $ax^2 + bx + c = 0$ where a, b, and c are numbers, ax^2 represents the square, bx represents the root, and c represents the number. The six forms Al-Khwarizmi allowed were:

1) Squares equal to roots or $ax^2 = bx$

This would be an equation like $x^2 = 4x$ which gives an answer of 4; and $3x^2 = 7x$ which gives an answer of $\frac{7}{3}$. These solutions are quite elementary when studied more closely. If we take the second example and divide both sides by 3 we get $x^2 = \frac{7}{3}x$ and since x^2 or $x \bullet x$ is on the left and $\frac{7}{3}x$ or $\frac{7}{3} \bullet x$ is on the right then:

$$x \bullet x = \frac{7}{3} \bullet x$$

and the first x on the left must be $\frac{7}{3}$. It's interesting to note that the first obvious solution for x is not given, namely $x = 0$.

2) Squares equal to numbers or $ax^2 = c$

"al-jabr"

Though I can't find any reference to show Al-Khwarizmi's method, a simple approach would be to isolate the x by dividing both sides by a and determining the square root by some method, possibly something similar to Archimedes' method.

3) Roots equal to numbers or $bx = c$

(See pages 26–7for solving linear equations.)

4) Squares and roots equal numbers or $ax^2 + bx = c$

5) Squares and numbers equal roots or $ax^2 + c = bx$

6) Roots and numbers equal squares or $bx + c = ax^2$

According to American historian of mathematics, Carl Boyer (1906–76), writing in *A History of Mathematics* (1968), for these three last examples: "The solutions are 'cookbook' rules for 'completing the square' applied to specific instances." We've already solved quadratics by completing the square on pages 72–3 and 76–7.

Exercise 14

Using the Quadratic Formula

THE PROBLEM:

Art and Paul have dug a parabolic swimming pool in both their backyards. The equation of the swimming pool is $6x^2 + 5x - 21 = d$, where d is the depth below the ground and x is the number of meters away from the property line. How far does the pool extend into each property?

THE METHOD

This problem will now be solved using the quadratic formula. From the ancient Egyptians onward it has been necessary to work with problems involving areas, and quadratic equations have been known since this time.

However, it was with Eastern mathematics that it began to take on a more modern form. As we've already seen, Al-Khwarizmi had six methods for solving various quadratics, then Sridhara was one of the first to produce a general formula for solving quadratics. However, although his form of the quadratic formula was brought to Europe, it wasn't quite like the one we know today. We have to wait a few centuries until European mathematicians led by Girolamo Cardano (who we'll meet later on pages 102–3) began to work with a full range of solutions that included complex and imaginary numbers (see pages 104–13). In 1637, when René Descartes published *La Géométrie*, the quadratic formula had adopted the form we know today.

The quadratic equation, or formula, is a generalized solution to any quadratic equation. It's really quite easy to use and the biggest mistakes tend to be simple errors in calculations rather than problems with understanding.

Yet again, with cunning brilliance, I have changed the nature of the problem entirely. I mean, really the problem is the same, and I suppose we'll solve it in a different way; but the real question is, who are Art and Paul?

Turn to pages 86–7 for information on Al-Khwarizmi.

The quadratic formula is:

$$x = \frac{-b \pm \sqrt{b^2 - 4ac}}{2a}$$

Where a, b, and c represent the coefficients in $ax^2 + bx + c = 0$.

So, for our problem: $a = 6$, $b = 5$, and $c = -21$ (don't forget the negative) after we plug in the variables, the formula becomes:

$$x = \frac{-(5) \pm \sqrt{(5)^2 - 4(6)(-21)}}{2(6)}$$

$$x = \frac{-5 \pm \sqrt{25 + 504}}{12}$$

$$x = \frac{-5 \pm \sqrt{529}}{12}$$

$$x = \frac{-5 \pm 23}{12}$$

Next we need to calculate both options:

$$x = \frac{-5 + 23}{12} \qquad x = \frac{-5 - 23}{12}$$

$$x = \frac{18}{12} \qquad x = \frac{-28}{12}$$

$$x = \frac{3}{2} \qquad x = \frac{-7}{3}$$

THE SOLUTION:

The solution is $x = \frac{3}{2}$ and $x = \frac{-7}{3}$ so the pool extends $\frac{-7}{3}$ of a meter (2.33 m) into Art's yard (I am assuming his house was to the left or negative side of the number line) and $\frac{3}{2}$ of a meter (1.5 m) into Paul's yard.

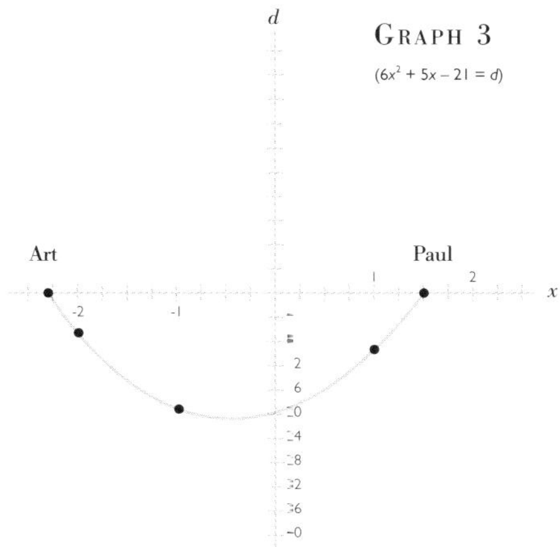

GRAPH 3

($6x^2 + 5x - 21 = d$)

• Here you can see a graph of the parabola that describes Art and Paul's swimming pool. You'll note that we've made the values of the d-axis positive because we worked with positive values for depth rather than "negative height." This is simply to make the graph easier to understand.

Profile

Omar Khayyam

Omar Khayyam was the first non-European mathematician I became aware of. From this point my Eurocentric ideas started to change, though from the contents of this book I'm sure you can see there is still room for improvement.

• Omar Khayyam The Persian mathematician who played a key role in the development of algebra.

Omar Khayyam was born on May 18, 1048 in Nishapur, Persia. Before the age of twenty-five, Khayyam had already produced significant works in mathematics. In 1070, he moved to Samarkand, in modern-day Uzbekistan, where he was supported by Abu Tahir, a prominent jurist. This allowed Khayyam to write his most important work: *Treatise on Demonstration of Problems of Algebra*. In 1073 Malik-Shah, sultan of the Seljuk dynasty, invited Khayyam to the city of Esfahan, the capital, to set up an observatory. Khayyam remained in Esfahan for the next 18 years. In 1092, after the death of Malik-Shah, political unrest ensued until 1118 when Malik-Shah's third son Sanjar assumed control of the Seljuk Dynasty. Sanjar moved the dynasty's capital to Merv, and Khayyam moved there sometime after 1118. In Merv, another center for learning was created, and Khayyam continued to work on his mathematics, until he died on December 4, 1122.

Major Works

• The Rubaiyat
Khayyam is probably best known through the Rubaiyat of Omar Khayyam, *a translation by Edward Fitzgerald. The* Rubaiyat *is a collection of 600 quatrains (four-line poems).*

• Problems of Arithmetic
A book on algebra and music. At the request of Malik-Shah, Khayyam set up an observatory in Esfahan. He calculated the length of a year to be 365.24219858156 days, which is amazingly accurate. He also created a new calendar, the Jalali calendar.

• Commentaries on the Difficult Postulate of Euclid's
Analyzing Euclid's parallel postulate, Khayyam made inroads into non-Euclidean geometry, although some claim that these were unintentional.

• Problems of Algebra (lost)
In his other works, Khayyam makes reference to a lost work in which he writes about what would later become known as Pascal's triangle (see pages 130–1 and 134–5).

CONICS

Conics is a section of mathematics that deals with shapes that can be drawn from a cone. There are four shapes that can be created from a cone. They are: the circle, the ellipse, the parabola, and the hyperbola.

These shapes show up all the time. The circle is an obvious case, it's pretty tough to have an automotive industry without circular tires. Meanwhile, an example of the ellipse is the path the Earth follows around the Sun; an example of a parabola (spun in three dimensions) is a satellite dish; while the shadow cast by a lampshade on a wall is a hyperbola.

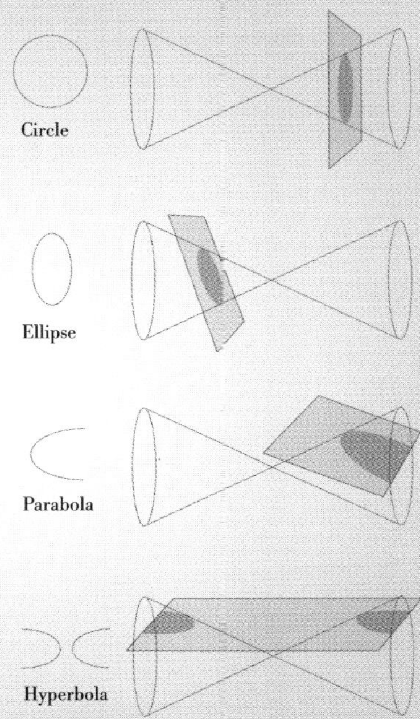

The Problems of Algebra

Treatise on Demonstration of Problems of Algebra is Omar Khayyam's greatest mathematical work. In this book, written in 1070, Khayyam outlines a complete classification of cubic equations with solutions found by using conics (see box above).

By finding the intersection point of two conics by geometric means, Khayyam was able to solve cubic equations. However, it's interesting to note that he only found one or maybe two of the three possible solutions. His solutions were geometric in nature, but Khayyam hoped that one day an arithmetical solution would be developed. This occurred many centuries later in the works of Italian mathematicians.

"The majority of people who imitate philosophers confuse the true with the false, and they do nothing but deceive and pretend knowledge, and they do not use what they know of the sciences except for base and material purposes."

Treatise on Demonstration of Problems of Algebra

Chapter

4

The Italian Connection

As the center of mathematics moved toward the West, Italian mathematicians played a crucial role in its development—both in bringing it to Europe in the first place, then developing it during the Renaissance. In this chapter we will meet such beautiful and creative mathematics as the Fibonacci sequence, revisit the golden ratio, and find ourselves in the strange company of imaginary and complex numbers.

Profile

Fibonacci PART I

Although Archimedes, Gauss, and Newton are generally considered the "big three" of mathematics, there are two other mathematicians that are, in my opinion at least, more fun and accessible. These two mathematicians are Pascal, who we will meet in the next chapter, and Fibonacci, whose famous sequence we can see all around us.

Early Life

Fibonacci, also known as Leonardo Pisano (Leonardo of Pisa), was born in Pisa, Italy in 1170. Although he was born in Italy, Fibonacci was actually raised and educated in North Africa. His father Guilielmo was a diplomat for the Republic of Pisa, representing merchants who traded through a port in what is now Algeria.

Being educated in what was then part of the Islamic empire introduced Fibonacci to a number system vastly superior to that which was used in Europe at the time. During his life, Fibonacci witnessed the fall of the Abbasid Dynasty. An-Nasir was the thirty-fourth Abbasid Caliph who reigned from 1180 to 1225, and is considered the last strong Abbasid Caliph. During this time most of Spain and Portugal were conquered by the Christians. The Abbasid Dynasty ended in 1258 with the sacking of Baghdad.

Fibonacci traveled widely until 1200 when he returned to Pisa. During his time there, Fibonacci wrote several texts including *Liber Abaci* (1202), *Practica Geometriae* (1220), *Flos* (1225), and *Liber Quadratorum.* (1225). He also wrote other material but it has since been lost. Fibonacci died in 1250 in Pisa. Today a statue of him can be found in the cemetery near the Leaning Tower of Pisa.

Practica Geometriae and Flos

Practica Geometriae is eight chapters of geometry problems based on Euclid's *Elements* and *On Division of Figures*. Fibonacci also includes a chapter detailing how to find the height of tall objects using similar triangles (see page 38). In *Flos*, Fibonacci solves a cubic equation previously solved by Omar Khayyam (see pages 90–1) and though the solution is irrational, Fibonacci managed to get the answer correct to nine decimal places.

Liber Quadratorum

Liber Quadratorum (*Book of Squares*) is considered by some to be Fibonacci's best work, though it's not as famous as *Liber Abaci*. It's a text on number theory, so the practical applications aren't obvious, but the mathematics is fascinating nonetheless.

In *Liber Quadratorum* Fibonacci looks at square numbers (see page 16), among other things, and wrote that they are the sums of odd numbers. That is to say:

$1 = 1$ (one is a square number)
$1 + 3 = 4$ (four is a square number)
$1 + 3 + 5 = 9$ (nine is a square number), and so on.

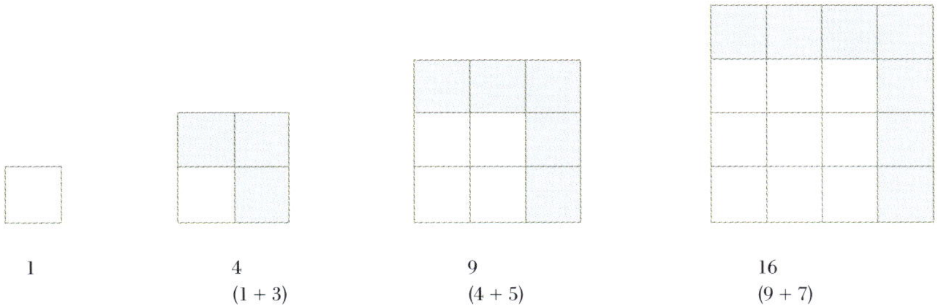

• **The first four square numbers. By observation we see that Fibonacci's idea that square numbers are the sums of odd numbers holds true.**

The diagram above shows that this holds true for the first few square numbers, but it would be good if we could show it was true of any square number. If we have a large square that measures n by n and we add to the sides and top corner more squares measuring one-by-one we get a square measure $(n + 1)$ by $(n + 1)$. The number of one-by-one squares added is $2n + 1$ which is an odd number.

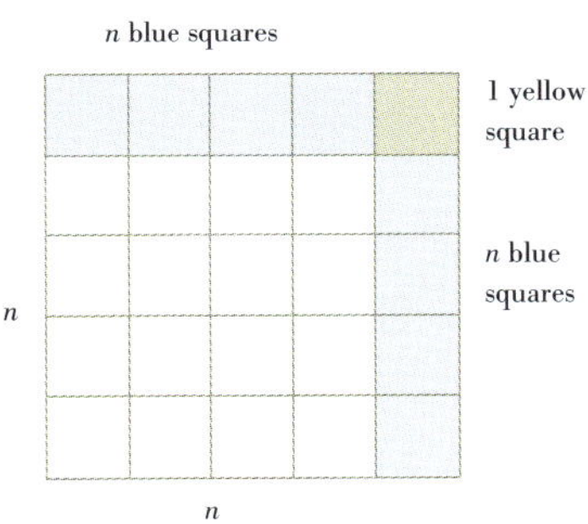

• **Proof of an idea requires that it always works. Although four squares are shown for n, n can represent any natural number. Use of a variable, in this case n, generalizes the solution.**

Therefore to increase for any square number n^2 to the next square number $(n + 1)^2$ you must add $n + n + 1$ or $2n + 1$. Therefore:

$$n^2 + 2n + 1 = (n + 1)^2$$

This can be solved by "foiling" out $(n + 1)^2$—see pages 34–5. The important part is the addition of $2n + 1$ to the n^2. Given that n can be any natural number, $2n$ is guaranteed to be an even number because it's a multiple of two. This means that $2n + 1$ must be odd. If we start with $n = 1$, the first square number, we see from the formula that we will get all successive odd numbers as n increases.

Fibonacci also writes about a way to find Pythagorean triples, which we also met earlier (see page 45). The first step is to take any odd square number as one of the shorter sides of a right-angled triangle. The other short side will be the sum of all the odd natural numbers up to the odd number chosen in the first step. Then you can sum these two numbers to complete a Pythagorean triple.

For example, take 25 as the first side. The sum of the odd natural numbers less than 25 is 144. Add 25 and 144 and you get 169, this can also be expressed as squares.

$$25 + 144 = 169 \text{ or } 5^2 + 12^2 = 13^2$$

GRAPHING PARABOLAS

To carry on our work with quadratics from the previous chapter, we'll now look at the graphical representation of a quadratic, the parabola. We can see parabolas in many places in the real world, for example the path a projectile follows is a parabola, if we ignore air resistance, and a satellite dish is the parabola that is perhaps closest to home.

Graphing the Parabola

The basic quadratic equation is $y = x^2$. The graph of this equation can be found by substituting a value for x so we can find the value of y. For example, when $x = -2$ the corresponding y value is 4, in other words $(-2)^2$, or $-2 \cdot -2$. This produces graph 4 (below).

From the bottom (vertex) of the parabola we go one unit left and right then up one to get two more points on the graph. Again from the vertex, we go out left and right two and up four to get another two points. This squaring continues indefinitely. In all of these graphs we represent this by marking the changing values in the tables with points on the graph, but continuing the line to show that its shape remains the same.

Moving a parabola around a piece of graph paper is relatively easy. Let's look at the graphs of the basic parabola, $y = x^2$, and two others: $y = x^2 + 3$ and $y = x^2 - 3$. If we made a table of values for these three functions we would notice that the +3 and the −3 just increase and decrease the y values and therefore move the parabola either up or down. That is to say that, given a graph of $y = x^2 \pm q$, the q value simply moves the parabola up or down (graph 5).

GRAPH 4

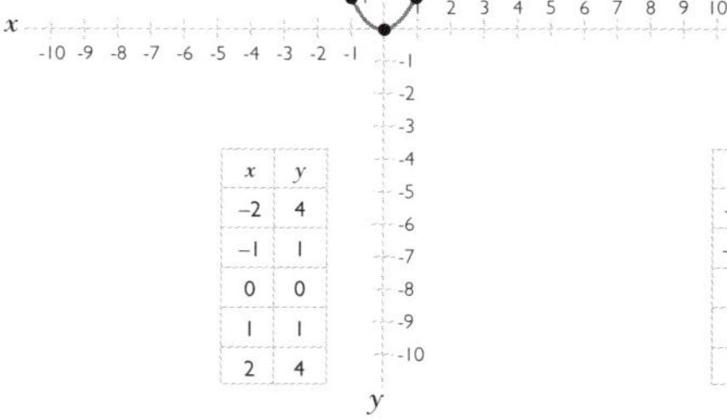

x	y
−2	4
−1	1
0	0
1	1
2	4

GRAPH 5

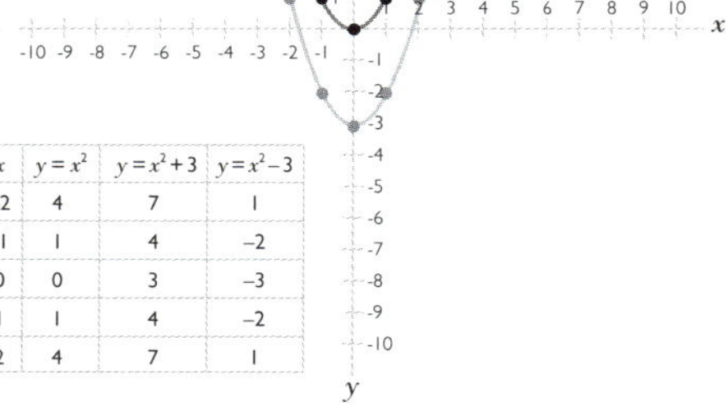

x	$y=x^2$	$y=x^2+3$	$y=x^2-3$
−2	4	7	1
−1	1	4	−2
0	0	3	−3
1	1	4	−2
2	4	7	1

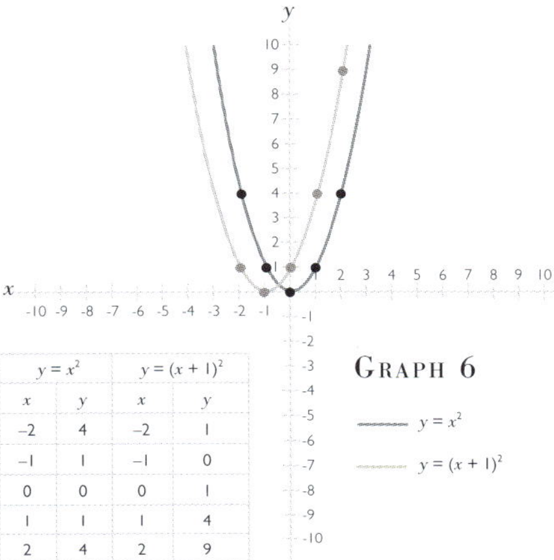

GRAPH 6

— $y = x^2$

— $y = (x + 1)^2$

$y = x^2$		$y = (x + 1)^2$	
x	y	x	y
−2	4	−2	1
−1	1	−1	0
0	0	0	1
1	1	1	4
2	4	2	9

Moving the graph left and right is a little more complicated. Starting with the basic parabola, $y = x^2$, we will shift the curve left and right by adding and subtracting numbers within the square; for example, graph 6 (above) shows the graph of our basic parabola $y = x^2$ and also the graph of $y = (x + 1)^2$, which is shifted to the left. The opposite occurs if we subtract values inside the bracket, for example, $y = (x - 1)^2$ in graph 7 (below) shifts the graph to the right.

GRAPH 7

— $y = x^2$

— $y = (x - 1)^2$

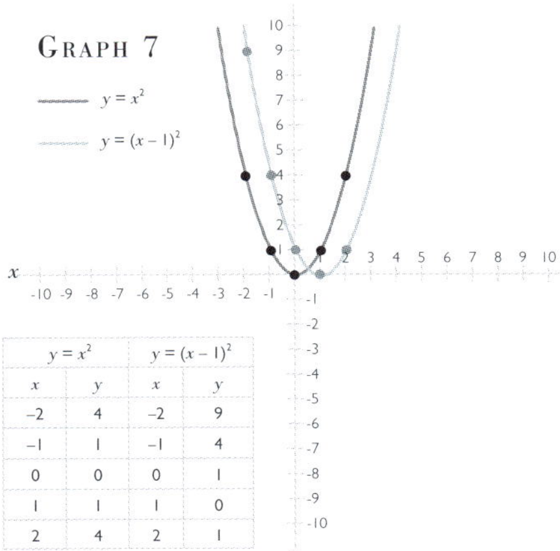

$y = x^2$		$y = (x - 1)^2$	
x	y	x	y
−2	4	−2	9
−1	1	−1	4
0	0	0	1
1	1	1	0
2	4	2	1

So if we have an equation in the form $y = (x \mp p)^2$, we know that the p moves the parabola left and right.

At this point a question usually arises: Why does the q variable do what it says, when the p variable does the opposite? That is to say, why does a positive q variable shift the curve in a positive direction (up); when a positive p variable shifts the curve in a negative direction (left)—and vice versa?

The answer is surprisingly straightforward. It's just to do with the way we like to write our equations. Really an equation of the form $y = x^2 - q$ should be written as $y + q = x^2$, but we tend to write our equations in the form "$y = \ldots$"

That said, the reason isn't too vital, it's just a question of getting your head around this quirk. Once you understand that, it's pretty simple to start drawing graphs of equations that are presented in the form $y = (x \mp p)^2 \pm q$. It's made even easier because the p and q variables don't affect each other—q just cares about up or down and nothing else, p cares about left and right and that's it. Just remember: positive q shifts up, positive p shifts left.

So what are you going to do with your newfound ability to graph a parabola? Well, as we mentioned on page 84, they can be used in any number of real-world applications, and as graphs they're exceptionally useful for modeling everything from motion, through business and economic systems, to demographics. In addition, they make for great reflectors, and are used in the headlamps of your car—it's the parabola that focuses the beam further ahead.

Profile # Fibonacci Part II

***Liber Abaci*, not to be confused with the flamboyant pianist Liberace, is Fibonacci's most famous work. Written in 1202, it's to this work that Western mathematics owes its renaissance. Through *Liber Abaci*, Fibonacci introduced Hindu–Arabic numerals to Europe thus making arithmetic much easier.**

The Modern Number System

The Hindu-Arabic number system has a long and storied past. Its beauty lies in the fact that it's a base-ten positional system that allows for easy arithmetic. It began in India, and in the seventh century, Brahmagupta formulated the first mathematical concepts that treat zero as a number, not just a place holder.

These ideas flowed westward through the Islamic empire. They were passed on by Al-Khwarizmi in the early ninth century and then on to Fibonacci. Though *Liber Abaci* was not the first text to introduce Hindu-Arabic numerals to Europe, it was the first to catch on. This can be attributed to the practical nature of its presentation and the benefits Fibonacci clearly saw in the system. The first section dealt with the arithmetic of the Hindu-Arabic system and the second section dealt with problems confronted by merchants.

The Fibonacci Sequence

In the third section of the book, a problem dealing with rabbits introduced what would become known as the Fibonacci Sequence. The problem went something like this:

A man starts with a pair of bunnies (one male, one female). It takes one month for them to mature to the point when they can breed. Then it takes one month for impregnation, pregnancy, and birth. Each birth produces one male and one female. How many pairs of rabbits will you have at the end of each month?

To start, the man has one pair. At the start of the next month he will still have one pair, but they will be mature. At the start of month three he will have two pairs: the original and the newborn pair. Note that the original pair will begin to produce again while the newborn pair needs one month to grow up. At the start of

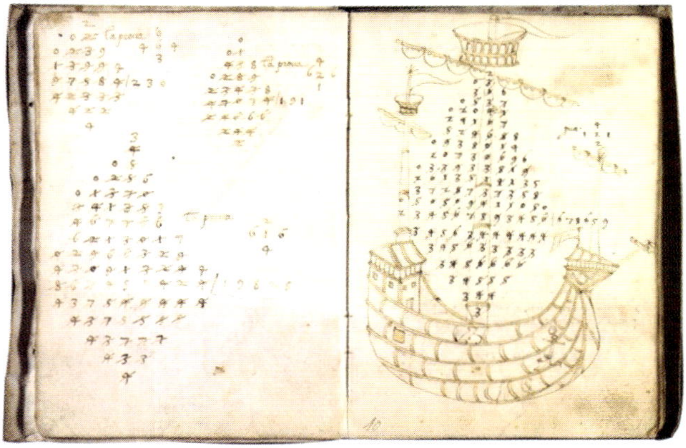

• Although *Liber Abaci* is known for introducing Hindu-Arabic numerals and the Fibonacci sequence, it was also directed at merchants and the finance of trade.

the fourth month he will have three pairs: the original, the first generation (which is ready to breed), and a new pair of bunnies. At the start of month five we have five pairs of rabbits because there are now two pairs giving birth.

Mathematically the formula for finding the numbers in a Fibonacci sequence is $f_{n+2} = f_{n+1} + f_n$ which looks weird but just means that the new Fibonacci number (f_{n+2}), is the sum of the two preceding Fibonacci numbers $f_{n+1} + f_n$. The first few terms in the sequence are: 1, 1, 2, 3, 5, 8, 13, 21, 34, 55, 89, and so on.

• The Fibonacci sequence occurs in many places in nature. In this case, there are twenty-one petals on the daisy.

THE FIBONACCI SEQUENCE IN NATURE

Fibonacci numbers can be found all through nature. There are many flowers that have petals which match Fibonacci numbers. Here is a short list:

3 petals: lily, iris

5 petals: buttercup, wild rose, larkspur, columbine (aquilegia)

8 petals: delphiniums

13 petals: daisies, ragwort, corn marigold, cineraria

21 petals: daisies, aster, black-eyed susan, chicory

34 petals: daisies, plantain, pyrethrum

55, 89 petals: michaelmas daisies, the *asteraceae* family

THE GOLDEN RATIO

Some numbers are just cool. Earlier I wrote about my π shirt, but there are plenty of other groovy numbers as well. Here we're going to take a look at phi (φ), which is one of the most beautiful and fascinating numbers of all.

The Golden Ratio

The value of phi (φ), also known as the golden ratio or section, is $\frac{1+\sqrt{5}}{2}$. This might seem like a weird number, but like the other cool numbers, it tends to pop up all over the place. Some say that its appearance is just a coincidence and that if you look for something you're sure to find it. I think these people miss out on the joys of life.

Like π, φ is an irrational number meaning that if you try to write it as a decimal you will be busy for a very long time indeed! However, just to give the first few decimal places, the value of the golden ratio is roughly 1.618033989.

It's here that things get interesting, as when we chart the Fibonacci numbers and divide one number by its immediate predecessor, the result starts to approach the golden ratio.

f_n	$f_n \div f_{n-1}$
1	N/A
1	1
2	2
3	1.5
5	1.666667
8	1.6
13	1.625
...	...

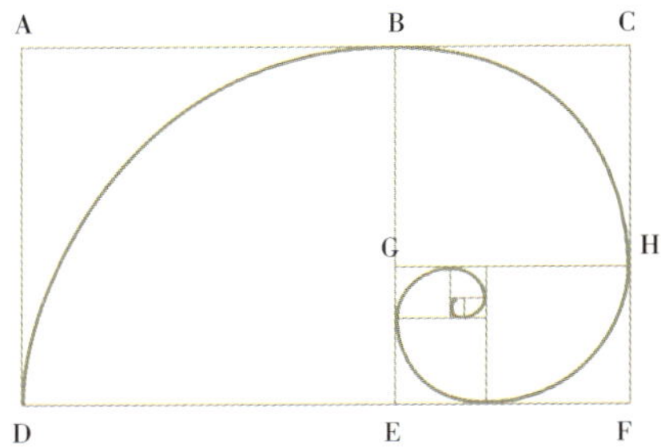

• The rectangle above (ACFD) is a golden rectangle; the ratio of its sides AC/CF is the golden ratio. If we remove the square ABED a new rectangle is formed (BCFE), which is also golden. If we remove the square BCHG we find yet another golden rectangle (GHFE), and so on. Drawing a curve from corner to opposite corner of each box creates a "golden spiral."

Finding the Golden Ratio

Using the Fibonacci sequence is just one way to find the value of φ. The golden ratio is $\frac{1+\sqrt{5}}{2}$, but it can also be written as a repeating fraction (the three dots mean that the fractions go on forever).

$$1+\cfrac{1}{1+\cfrac{1}{1+\cfrac{1}{1+\cfrac{1}{\ddots}}}}$$

We can see the convergence to φ by ignoring parts of the repeating fraction and just using the beginning parts.

First term = 1

Second term = 1+ 1 = 2

$$\text{Third term} = 1 + \frac{1}{1+1} = 1 + \frac{1}{2} = 1.5$$

Now this could get torturous, some might say it already has, but it's easier if we realize the denominator is just the previous term. So the fourth term is:

$$1 + \frac{1}{\text{third term}} = 1 + \frac{1}{1.5} = 1.6$$

If we continued we'd find ourselves again converging on the golden ratio. And the same is true when φ is expressed as a repeating square root.

$$\varphi = \sqrt{1+\sqrt{1+\sqrt{1+\sqrt{1+\ldots}}}}$$

Yet another interesting property of φ is that its reciprocal $(\frac{1}{\varphi})$ is equal to one less than φ or $\frac{1}{\varphi} = \varphi - 1$.

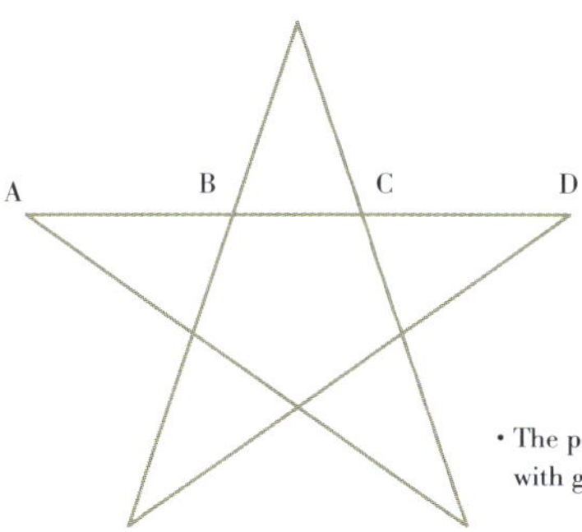

• The pentagram is filled with golden ratios.

• Though I'm no *Vitruvian Man*, the height to my navel is 44 in and my total height is 72 in—a ratio of 1.636. Pretty close to the golden ratio.

The Golden Ratio in Life

The golden ratio can be found throughout nature. In the human body, given the slightly unreasonable assumption that you have the perfect figure, we find the ratio in: your overall height divided by the height to your navel; the ratios of the lengths of the bones in your fingers; the ratio of the length from your elbow to your wrist to the length of your hand.

In fact, φ, or the golden ratio, shows up wherever the Fibonacci sequence can be seen. There are many examples of it in nature, and it can also be found in the art and architecture of humankind, for example, the proportions of the *Mona Lisa* or the *Parthenon* in Athens.

In one final example, the golden ratio also can be found in the lines of a pentagram. On the diagram to the left, the ratios of certain lengths, for example, $\frac{AD}{AC}$, $\frac{AC}{AB}$, and $\frac{AB}{BC}$, are all the golden ratio.

Profile

Tartaglia and Cardano

Fast-forward some two hundred and fifty years and quadratics have become old hat. Mathematicians had more or less got their heads around them and mathematics had moved on. In Italy, in the 1500s, cubic equations were where it was at. Today cubic equations are involved in all sorts of applications, particularly those that involve volumes.

Niccolo Tartaglia

Niccolo Fontana Tartaglia was born in Brescia, Italy, which at the time was part of the Republic of Venice. The year was 1499 or 1500. Tartaglia's father was the sixteenth-century equivalent of a postal worker, riding from town to town making deliveries. This provided a meager existence, but when Tartaglia was only six, his father was murdered, sending him and his family into poverty. Then things went from bad to worse; in 1512 the French invaded the town and slaughtered its people. Tartaglia was cut by a French soldier, leaving him with a damaged jaw and palate. This was the reason he wore a large beard and had difficulty speaking. All in all he had a rough childhood.

However, due to Tartaglia's ability in mathematics, his mother found him a patron and he went to study in Padua, Italy. He returned to Brescia for a short while before moving to Verona in 1516 to teach mathematics. Then, in 1534, he moved to Venice to teach. From this time until his death in 1557, Tartaglia was involved in a series of arguments with other Italian mathematicians.

•Niccolo Tartaglia

Girolamo Cardano

Girolamo Cardano was born in Pavia, Northern Italy in 1501. He was the illegitimate son of Fazio Cardano and Chiara Micheria. His father Fazio was a lawyer but because of his skills in mathematics he lectured on geometry at the University of Pavia and the Piatti Foundation in Milan. Cardano's father also consulted with Leonardo da Vinci on problems in geometry.

Cardano's first job was that of an assistant to his father. However, Cardano aspired to greater things and fought with his father. He entered medical school in Pavia and was very successful, although he made many enemies due to his abrasive demeanor. He received his doctorate of medicine in 1525, but his outspoken nature made it difficult for him to be admitted to the College of Physicians in Milan and it would be fourteen years before he gained entry.

He married in 1531, and during the 14 years between his degree and his admission to the College of Physicians in Milan, Cardano attempted to make a life as a physician in a small village, gambling (dice, cards, and chess), and lecturing mathematics at the Piatti Foundation, like his father before him. In 1539 Cardano started his correspondence with Tartaglia, and the rest of his life was filled with controversy.

It wasn't just mathematical problems that engulfed Cardano's life. His oldest son was convicted of the murder of his wife and executed. His youngest son was a gambler, and not a good one—he gambled away most of his possessions and much of Cardano's money. Then in 1570 Cardano was accused of heresy for having published a horoscope of Jesus over a decade earlier, and was put in jail for several months on the strength of evidence that included his own son's. Cardano moved to Rome, where he died in 1576.

Tartaglia Takes on the World

Scipione del Ferro, an Italian mathematician who was born in Bologna in 1465, is credited with being the first to solve cubic equations. He kept his process or formula for solving these equations under wraps until 1526 when, on his death bed he revealed his secret to his student, Antonio Fior.

Fior boasted that he could solve cubics and after some mathematical "trash talk" he and Tartaglia set about what amounted to a mathematical duel. Each would give the other thirty problems to be solved over a period of time. To kick things off, Fior gave Tartaglia thirty problems of the form $x^3 + ax = b$. Tartaglia, however, knew how to solve equations of the form $x^3 + ax^2 = b$. At the beginning of the competition Tartaglia couldn't solve Fior's problems, but one morning he had a breakthrough and solved them all in less than two hours. He was now able to solve cubics in both forms. The problems Tartaglia set in return were more varied and Fior lost the competition.

At this point Cardano became interested in cubic equations and wrote to ask Tartaglia for his method. Tartaglia refused, but this didn't disuade Cardano who continued to press the issue. Over the course of many letters, he ground Tartaglia into submission, and persuaded him to reveal his method on the promise that Cardano never reveal it to anyone else and would only keep the information in code.

On the basis of that understanding, Cardano and his assistant Ferrari continued working on cubic and quartic equations. But in 1543 Cardano discovered that del Ferro was actually the first to solve cubic equations, and no longer felt obliged to honor his promise to Tartaglia. Consequently, he published *Ars Magna* in 1545, which included methods for solving cubic equations both from del Ferro and Tartaglia, as well as the advances that Cardano and Ferrari had made themselves.

Tartaglia was none too happy and published his side of the story along with a few personal attacks. However, they failed to have the desired impact and Cardano's reputation as a leading mathematician was largely untouched.

Things came to a head when Ferrari, Cardano's assistant, challenged Tartaglia to a public debate. Tartaglia was initially reluctant because beating a relative unknown would do little to raise his stature, but losing could be very damaging. However, after trading insults with Ferrari for a year, he finally accepted. Tartaglia was the hot favorite, but after the first day it seemed Ferrari was likely to win. With no stomach for the fight, Tartaglia left that night, and his absence the next day gave Ferrari his victory.

IMAGINARY AND COMPLEX NUMBERS

New number types have caused controversy throughout the ages. (To review number types or sets see pages 14–17.) As new problems are discovered, their solutions often require new mathematics, and with this new mathematics come new number types. Imaginary and complex numbers are great examples of this; but before we look at them more closely let's review the development of our number system.

Imaginary numbers, and by extension complex numbers, have many applications. Complex numbers are needed when working with electromagnetic fields and alternating current (AC) circuits. Quantum mechanics and even those cool fractal posters require complex numbers as well. Control systems and signal analysis also require complex numbers.

Controversy in the Past

During the time of Pythagoras we had the natural numbers (1, 2, 3, and so on) and we had positive fractions or rational numbers. Then, when the Pythagoreans discovered irrational numbers they got quite upset. The idea of a number that can't be expressed as a fraction was just too dangerous.

Now, however, we see irrational numbers as an important part of mathematics—how else would you solve $x^2 = 2$? And eventually the Greeks became accustomed to the idea.

Zero also caused a lot of problems over the ages. It should be pointed out that we're talking about zero the number not zero the place holder—yes, there is a difference. For many years the idea of zero as a place holder existed, but not as a number itself.

To the Greeks, who looked upon mathematics from a geometric perspective, zero seemed absurd or unnecessary. When numbers or unknowns represented lengths, and squares represented areas, zero had no place. Why solve a problem that did not exist? If a length is zero there is no line; if an area is zero there is no object. It was Brahmagupta (see pages 78–9) who tried to place zero within the rules of arithmetic.

Negative numbers also suffered along with zero. In fact acceptance of negative numbers took a little longer. Zero had the advantage of starting out as a place holder, but negative numbers did not. Again it was Brahmagupta who tried to bring negative numbers into the family. Although negative numbers gained acceptance in the East, European mathematicians continued to have trouble with them even during the sixteenth century when Italian mathematicians were starting to contemplate imaginary numbers.

• The Mandelbrot set is a fractal generated by a complex quadratic—all that really matters is how great it looks!

Imaginary and Complex Numbers

Let's begin by saying that "imaginary" is a bad label for this type of number. It implies that these numbers do not exist when they do. In fact, they are very real and very necessary in mathematics.

An imaginary number is just $\sqrt{-1}$ and is represented by the letter i or j—mathematicians use i while engineers tend to use j.

The use of imaginary numbers helps us solve some very simple-looking equations. If we had $x^2 - 1 = 0$ we could solve this by isolating x^2 and get $x^2 = 1$ and then $x = \pm 1$. This type of equation is easy to solve. If we change the problem slightly to $x^2 + 1 = 0$, and we isolate x^2 then we get $x^2 = -1$. This causes a bit of grief. What number, when squared, equals a negative number? Well, nothing unless you invent or discover a new number. This is how the imaginary number was born.

If we make $i = \sqrt{-1}$ then $i^2 = -1$ then the solution to the problem $x^2 + 1 = 0$ is $x = \pm i$. It doesn't matter if you don't understand right now, complex arithmetic is covered on pages 106–7.

Complex numbers, meanwhile, are just numbers that have both a real and imaginary component. For example, $3 + 4i$ is a complex number because the 3 can be considered a "real three" while the 4 is an imaginary number.

A LITTLE HISTORY

Just like irrational numbers, zero, and negative numbers, imaginary and complex numbers have caused their own controversy over the years. The first published account of complex numbers comes from Cardano's *Ars Magna* (see page 103). When solving cubic and quartic equations, Cardano came across the square root of a negative number in the middle of the calculation. Ignoring the fact that this was an "imaginary" or "impossible" situation he continued the calculation to produce a "real" result.

Rafael Bombelli (see page 111) was the first to work explicitly with complex numbers and wrote of operations with them in 1572. René Descartes (see pages 116–17) is sometimes credited with giving imaginary numbers their name in the seventeenth century, and two centuries later Carl Gauss (see pages 144–5) introduced the term "complex number."

COMPLEX ARITHMETIC

Complex arithmetic is not that complex really. In fact, all it requires is an understanding of the Cartesian coordinate system—graph paper to you and me—and a little trigonometry. It also requires that you accept the existence of imaginary numbers; if you can separate numbers from the physical world then that helps. There are, however, masses of real-world applications for complex numbers, including alternating-current (AC) circuits.

The Real Number Line

Let's start with the real number line, our old friend from when we were learning to count and do basic addition and subtraction by having the happy frog hop along the line. Now, if we place our frog at 4 on the number line then multiplying by -1 the frog will hop all the way across the number line, and land on -4. As the frog turned all the way around we can see that the angle of the hop was 180°. If we then multiply by -1 again we end up back at 4; that's another 180° turn, making a total of 360°. In both cases multiplying by -1 causes a hop of 180°.

Now we're going to add another axis to our number line. The horizontal axis represents the real numbers and the vertical axis represents the imaginary numbers (see above right).

Since $i = \sqrt{-1}$ we can think of i as half a negative sign. If we start our frog at 4 again and multiply by i, this moves the frog to $4i$ on the graph—the frog has hopped 90°, half the value it did for a multiplication by -1. If we then take this position $4i$ and multiply by i again we get $4i^2$. If $i = \sqrt{-1}$ then $i^2 = -1$ and $4i^2$ is equal to -4. This represents another hop of 90°. Therefore, when we multiply by -1 we hop 180° and when we multiply by i we hop 90°. If our frog started at 4 on the number line, and is then multiplied by i three times or i^3 it would hop through 270° and end up at $-4i$. This is because two of the three "i"s made the negative sign and left one extra i.

• Multiplying by -1 causes the frog to hop through 180°.

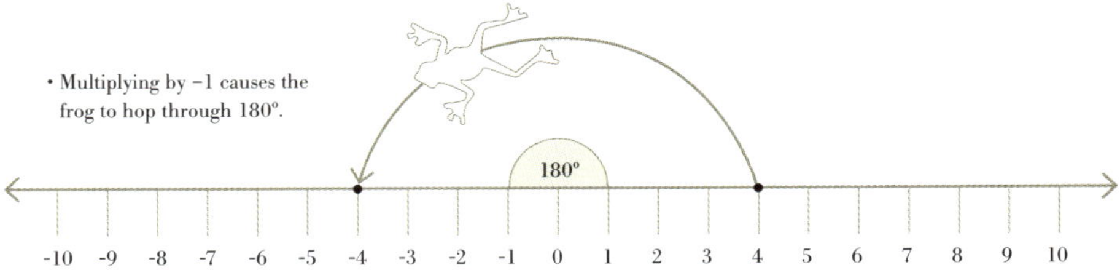

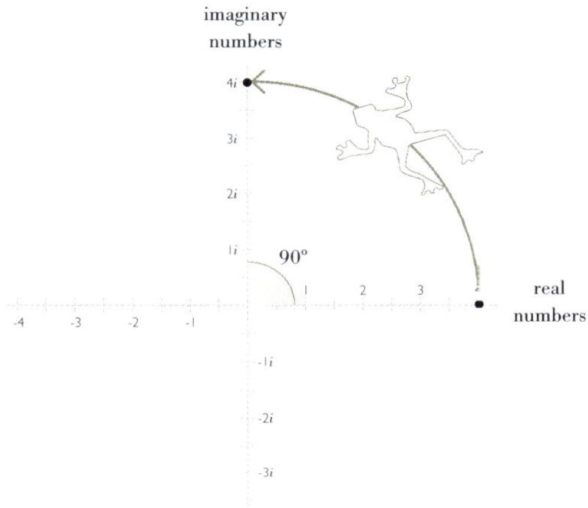

• Multiplying by i (which is half of -1) causes the frog to hop through 90°.

Complex Numbers

Complex numbers are numbers that have both real and imaginary components. To represent these numbers we can place them on the complex plain (our graph paper with a real and imaginary axis). If we have the number $(3 + 4i)$, it would be a point three to the right and four up. If we draw a line from the origin (where the vertical and horizontal lines meet) to the point, we can determine the length of the line using the Pythagorean theorem (see pages 44–5) and the angle the line makes with the positive real axis using trigonometry (see pages 38–9). Using the Pythagorean theorem $a^2 + b^2 = c^2$, where a and b are 3 and 4, we get $3^2 + 4^2 = c^2$ then $9 + 16 = c^2$ then $25 = c^2$ or $c = 5$. This represents the absolute value or modulus of the complex number. To find the angle we take the inverse tangent of $\frac{4}{3}$ or $\tan^{-1}(\frac{4}{3}) = \theta \approx 53°$.

Multiplying a Complex Number by *i*

Earlier we said that multiplying by i causes a rotation (or hop) of 90°. To demonstrate this let's multiply $(3 + 4i)$ by i. Given $i\,(3 + 4i)$, the i swoops in to give $3i + 4i^2$. As $4i^2$ is -4, the new complex number is $-4 + 3i$. This number is now in the upper left part of the graph paper.

Again, using the Pythagorean theorem, we find that the length of the line is five and using trigonometry we find the angle the line makes with the negative real axis. To find the angle we can take the inverse tangent of $\frac{3}{4}$ or $\tan^{-1}(\frac{3}{4}) = \theta \approx 37°$. If we look at the angle formed between the number $(3 + 4i)$ and $(-4 + 3i)$ we see that it's 90°. So multiplying by i rotated the point (line) by 90° but does not change the length. The next section will deal with multiplying and adding complex numbers.

Adding Complex Numbers

Adding complex numbers is quite easy; you just add the real parts together and then the imaginary parts together. For example, let's add $(3 + 4i) + (2 + 5i)$. This becomes $(5 + 9i)$.

Graphically we can look at this in two ways. In the first we draw the line for each complex number from the origin. The first number goes to the right three and the second number goes to the right two—the total distance is five. The first number goes up four and the second goes up five—the total distance is nine. The second approach is to use a tip-to-tail method (see graph 8). From the tip of the first number you place the tail of the second. So first you move to three right and four up, then from this point you move another two right and five up to finish five right and nine up.

GRAPH 8

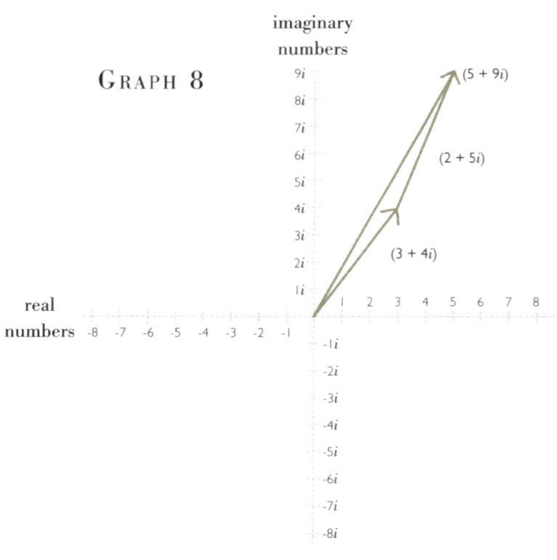

Multiplying Complex Numbers

Multiplying complex numbers is no different from multiplying binomials (see pages 34–5); complex numbers are just binomials with a real and imaginary part. As an example, let's multiply $(3 + 4i)(2+5i)$. Whenever we multiply two binomials we "foil":

$$(3 + 4i)(2+5i) = 6 + 15i + 8i + 20i^2$$
$$= 6 + 23i - 20 = -14+23i$$

Remember that $i^2 = -1$ so $20i^2$ is equal to $20(-1)$ or -20.

This can be demonstrated graphically (connecting the geometry to the algebra) by plotting the two binomials and the resulting binomial. We will do each step individually.

Graphing $(3 + 4i)$

If we plot $(3 + 4i)$ we have a point three to the right and four up. If we make a line from the origin and use the Pythagorean theorem, we find the length of this line is five:

$$3^2 + 4^2 = c^2 \text{ then}$$
$$9 + 16 = c^2 \text{ then}$$
$$25 = c^2 \text{ or } c = 5.$$

The angle can be found by using trigonometry (see page 39); we take the inverse tangent of $\frac{4}{3}$ or:

$$\tan^{-1}\left(\tfrac{4}{3}\right) = \theta \approx 53.13°$$

Graphing (2 + 5*i*)

If we plot $(2 + 5i)$ then we have a point that is two to the right and five up. If we make a line from the origin and use the Pythagorean theorem we find that the length of this line is $\sqrt{29}$ or approximately:

$$2^2 + 5^2 = c^2 \text{ then}$$
$$4 + 25 = c^2 \text{ then}$$
$$29 = c^2 \text{ or}$$
$$c = \sqrt{29} \text{ or } c = 5.3852$$

The angle can be found by using trigonometry; we take the inverse tangent of $\frac{5}{2}$ or $\tan^{-1}(\frac{5}{2}) = \theta \approx 68.20°$.

Graphing (−14 + 23*i*)

If we plot $(-14 + 23i)$ we have a point fourteen to the left and twenty-three up. If we make a line from the origin and use the Pythagorean theorem we find the length of this line is $\sqrt{725}$ or approximately 26.926:

$$(-14)^2 + 23^2 = c^2 \text{ then}$$
$$196 + 529 = c^2 \text{ then}$$
$$725 = c^2 \text{ or}$$
$$c = \sqrt{725} \text{ or } c = 26.926$$

The angle can be found by using trigonometry; we take the inverse tangent of $\frac{23}{14}$ or $\tan^{-1}(\frac{23}{14}) = \theta \approx 58.67°$.

This angle is the angle between the negative real axis and the line. To find the angle between the line and the positive real axis we subtract this angle from 180°. The angle from the positive real axis is 180° − 58.67° or 121.33°.

Bringing it Together

This length of the resultant binomial 26.926 represents the multiplication of the lengths of the two original binomials 5 and 5.3852. The angle of the resultant binomial (121.33°) is the sum of the angles that the two original binomials formed with the positive real axis. To view this graphically (see Graph 9, below), when you multiply two complex numbers you multiply their lengths and you add the angles they form with the positive real axis.

Complex number	Length	Angle
$(3 + 4i)$	5	53.13°
$(2 + 5i)$	5.3852	68.20°
$(-14 + 23i)$	26.926	121.33°

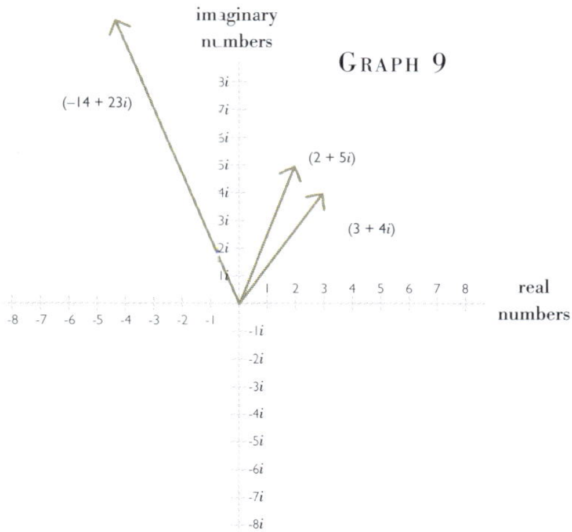

GRAPH 9

CONJUGATES

Conjugates are a nifty way to produce a real number from two complex numbers. Conjugates are complex numbers where the real parts are the same but the imaginary parts are negatives of each other. For example, $(3 + 4i)$ and $(3 - 4i)$ are conjugates. They are helpful because when you multiply conjugates the imaginary part disappears.

Let's start with the following expression:

$$(3 + 4i)(3 - 4i)$$

Which we can "foil" to give:

$$9 - 12i + 12i - 16i^2$$

Remember that $i^2 = -1$ so $-16i^2$ is equal to $-16(-1)$ or $+16$, and we can cancel out the $-12i$ and the $12i$ to give:

$$9 + 16 = 25.$$

When we multiply complex numbers we multiply the lengths and we add the angles (see pages 108–9). Looking at Graph 10 we can see that the first complex number has an angle of 53.13° above the positive real axis and the second complex number has an angle of 53.13° below the positive real axis. Adding these angles therefore gives 0° and produces a real number.

When solving polynomial equations with real coefficients, the solution sometimes includes complex numbers. When this happens the complex numbers come in pairs: one complex number and its conjugate.

GRAPH 10

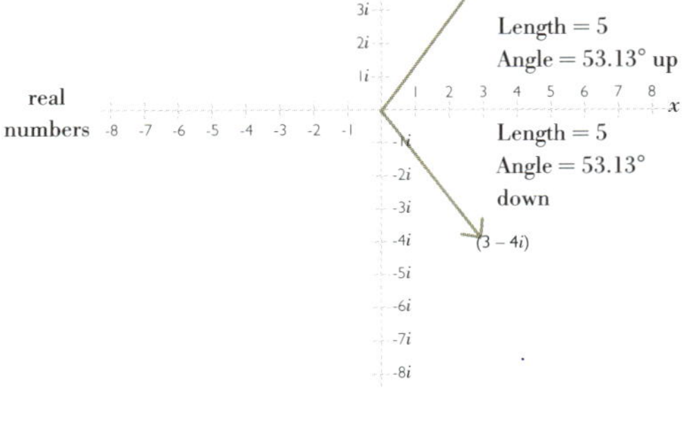

Conjugates Put to Work

To divide complex numbers is a little more complicated and requires the use of the conjugate. As an example, let's divide $\frac{(-8 + 3i)}{(3 + 2i)}$. First we multiply the top and bottom by the conjugate of the bottom, then "foil" out the top and bottom, then simplify, this gives a chain of equations as follows:

$$\frac{(-8+3i)}{(3+2i)} = \frac{(-8+3i)}{(3+2i)} \cdot \frac{(3-2i)}{(3-2i)} = \frac{-24+16i+9i-6i^2}{9-6i+6i-4i^2} =$$

$$\frac{-24+25i+6}{9+4} = \frac{-18+25i}{13} = \frac{-18}{13} + \frac{25i}{13}$$

so $\frac{(-8+3i)}{(3+2i)} = \frac{-18}{13} + \frac{25i}{13}$

Division follows the same graphical approach as multiplication. But when dividing complex numbers you divide their lengths and subtract their angles.

RAFAEL BOMBELLI

Rafael Bombelli was born in Bologna, Italy in 1526. Following on from Cardano and Tartaglia, he and Lodovico Ferrari, Cardano's assistant, represented the next generation of great mathematicians from northern Italy—the hub of mathematics at the time.

Bombelli's father was a wool merchant and consequently Bombelli didn't receive a university education. Instead he learned his mathematics from Pier Francesco Clementi, an architect and engineer.

Bombelli followed Clementi into the field of engineering, and began working on land-reclamation projects. But in 1555, when the project he was working on was suspended, Bombelli decided to write a comprehensive review of algebra with the aim of making the subject more accessible. However, Bombelli's day job recommenced in 1560, before he could finish his book. It would be nearly a decade before his writings would be published. However, this wasn't necessarily such a bad thing. Bombelli was invited to Rome to work on further engineering projects, and during his time there he was introduced to the work of the Greek mathematician Diophantus (see pages 64–5). Bombelli undertook to make a translation of Diophantus's *Arithmetica*, but although the work remained unfinished it greatly influenced his work on algebra.

When it was eventually published in three parts, Bombelli's *Algebra* included a number of problems he had taken from Diophantus. He intended to publish two further parts on geometry, but these remained unfinished when he died in 1572—although their manuscripts have since been discovered.

Bombelli's work was significant for two reasons: first his comfortable nature working with negative numbers; and second for laying down the rules of addition, subtraction, and multiplication of complex numbers.

QUADRATICS, PARABOLAS, AND COMPLEX NUMBERS

Quadratics are very important. Besides their use in expressing the force that keeps us all aboard our giant space marble (gravity), quadratics are useful in control systems everywhere from pulp mills to chemical plants.

It All Comes Together

In chapter three we met quadratics and solved them in many ways: by decomposition; by "BaRF" and "down under"; by completing the square; and by using the quadratic formula. Then, earlier in this chapter, we graphed parabolas and met complex arithmetic for the first time. Now we bring these ideas together.

When solving polynomials, in this case quadratics, we're looking for the value of x which makes the equation equal to zero. When we graph the quadratics (parabolas) we introduce the y variable to construct the graph.

A Quadratic with Two Solutions

To start, let's use a quadratic which would work nicely for mathematicians through the ages—positive whole number solutions. Let's analyze $0 = x^2 - 6x + 5$ in two different ways: by looking at the graph and by using the quadratic formula.

If we use the quadratic formula then we get:

$$\frac{-b \pm \sqrt{b^2 - 4ac}}{2a}$$

$$\frac{-(-6) \pm \sqrt{(-6)^2 - 4(1)(5)}}{2(1)}$$

$$\frac{6 \pm \sqrt{36 - 20}}{2}$$

$$\frac{6 \pm \sqrt{16}}{2}$$

$$\frac{6 \pm 4}{2}$$

which becomes $\frac{(6+4)}{2} = \frac{10}{2} = 5$ and $\frac{(6-4)}{2} = \frac{2}{2} = 1$.

So the solution to the polynomial equation $0 = x^2 - 6x + 5$ can be found by using the quadratic formula. These solutions also represent where the graph of $y = x^2 - 6x + 5$ crosses the x-axis.

A Quadratic with One Solution

Now let's analyze $0 = x^2 - 6x + 9$. If we use the quadratic formula we get:

$$\frac{-b \pm \sqrt{b^2 - 4ac}}{2a}$$

$$\frac{-(-6) \pm \sqrt{(6)^2 - 4(1)(9)}}{2(1)}$$

$$\frac{6 \pm \sqrt{36-36}}{2}$$

$$\frac{6 \pm \sqrt{0}}{2}$$

$$\frac{6 \pm 0}{2}$$

which becomes $\frac{(6+0)}{2} = \frac{6}{2} = 3$ and $\frac{(6-0)}{2} = \frac{6}{2} = 3$.

So the solution to the polynomial equation $0 = x^2 - 6x + 9$ can be found using the quadratic formula. These solutions also represent where the graph of $y = x^2 - 6x + 5$ meets the x-axis. In this case there are two equal solutions, so the graph just touches the x-axis.

A Quadratic with Imagination

Now let's analyze $0 = x^2 - 6x + 13$. If we use the quadratic formula we get:

$$\frac{-b \pm \sqrt{b^2 - 4ac}}{2a}$$

$$\frac{-(-6) \pm \sqrt{(-6)^2 - 4(1)(13)}}{2(1)}$$

$$\frac{6 \pm \sqrt{36-52}}{2}$$

$$\frac{6 \pm \sqrt{-16}}{2}$$

$$\frac{6 \pm 4i}{2}$$

which becomes $\frac{(6+4i)}{2}$ or $(3+2i)$ and $\frac{(6-4i)}{2}$ or $(3-2i)$.

So the solution to the polynomial equation can be found by using the quadratic formula. Because the graph does not cross the x-axis, there are no real solutions. The solutions now have an imaginary component and are complex. Notice that the solutions $(3+2i)$ and $(3-2i)$ are conjugates.

To Summarize

There is a connection between the equation, the solutions, and the graph—and these are shown below. When the value under the square root (called the discriminant) is positive, the equation has two distinct real solutions, so the parabola crosses the x-axis in two places. When the value of the square root is zero, the equation has two equal solutions, so the parabola just touches the x-axis. When the square root is negative, the solutions are complex numbers so the parabola does not touch the x-axis at all.

GRAPH 11

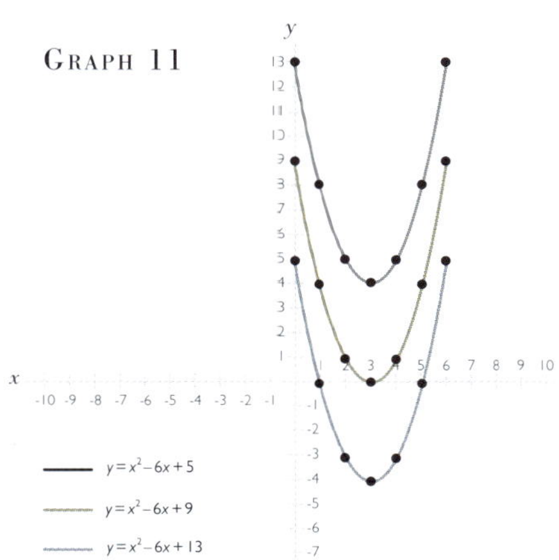

Chapter

5

Post-Renaissance Europe

As the Renaissance began to spread from Italy, Europe came alive with mathematical creativity. It was during this early modern period that some of the greatest mathematicians of all time lived: Pascal, Descartes, and Gauss. We shall meet some of these geniuses in this chapter, and with them one of the most beautiful mathematical constructions of all: Pascal's triangle.

Profile

René Descartes

If you try and look for the town of La Haye in France you will not find it. In its place you will find the town of Descartes. In 1802 La Haye changed its name to La Haye-Descartes in honor of René Descartes; then, in 1967 it dropped the La Haye altogether and simply became known as Descartes. Now, to have a street named after you is a pretty big deal, but to have your hometown change its name, that's something else. Granted, royals such as Queen Victoria and military conquerors such as Alexander the Great have this kind of thing happen all the time; but mathematicians are rarely so lucky.

Descartes was born in La Haye (now Descartes), France in 1596. When he was a baby his mother died of tuberculosis. At the age of eight he entered a Jesuit college in La Fleche, where he studied until the age of sixteen. During this time Descartes was in poor health and was given permission to stay in bed until late morning—a habit of sleeping in that he continued for most of his life. Some even say that when he stopped sleeping in, it caused his premature demise (see opposite). Descartes received a degree in law from the University of Poitiers in 1616. Shortly after this, he joined the army.

One story has it that in 1619, while walking through the streets of Breda, in the Netherlands, he came upon a poster written in Dutch and asked a passerby, in Latin, to translate it for him. The passerby was Isaac Beeckman, some eight years Descartes' senior and a Dutch philosopher and scientist in his own right. Beeckman agreed to translate the poster, which was a geometry problem, if Descartes would be willing to solve it. Of course, Descartes solved the problem in just a few hours and thus began a long friendship.

In the spring of 1621, around his twenty-fifth birthday, Descartes resigned from the army, and from then until 1628 he traveled throughout Europe. His travels took him to Bohemia, Hungary, Germany, Holland, France, then back to Holland in 1628.

Descartes in Holland

It was in Holland that Descartes produced the works that made him famous among both mathematicians and philosophers. Shortly after arriving there, Descartes was writing a book, *Le Monde* (*The World*), but after working on it for four long years, he decided not to publish. Why? Well, it seems that his reasoning was quite sound, given that he had just heard of Galileo's

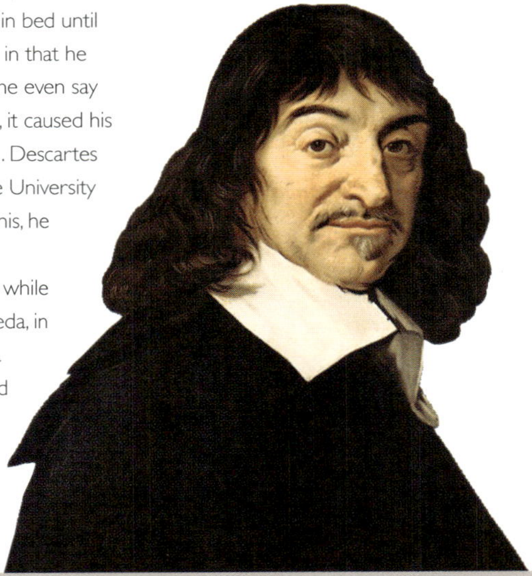

"Of all things, good sense is the most fairly distributed: everyone thinks he is so well supplied with it that even those who are the hardest to satisfy in every other respect never desire more of it than they already have."

Discours de la Méthode

subjection to house arrest in Italy for daring to challenge the Church's view of the universe.

Descartes' next work was *Discours de la Méthode Pour Bien Conduire sa Raison et Chercher la Verité dans les Sciences* or "*Discourse on the Method of Reasoning Well and Seeking Truth in the Sciences*," better known as *Discourse on Method*, which was published in 1637.

Discourse on Method

At the heart of *Discourse on Method* were Descartes' thoughts on what is true. In fact, it's in this work that we can find what is probably the most famous quote in philosophy: "Cogito ergo sum" or "I think, therefore I am," originally written as "Je pense donc je suis."

Discourse on Method has three appendices: "La Dioptrique," a work on optics, "Les Meteores," a work on meteorology, and "La Geometrie," a work on geometry.

"La Geometrie" is the most significant part of *Discourse on Method*. It's in this appendix that Descartes lays out the framework of analytic geometry. From this text we get the basis of our work in algebra, and it's at this point that students of today can read a work of algebra and not confront problems with notation. Descartes created a connection between geometry and algebra that we now take for granted. It's also interesting to note that it's from this appendix that we get the Cartesian coordinate system, or graph paper. (Cartesian simply means relating to Descartes, so it wasn't just a town that he had named after him!)

Getting Up Early Can Kill You

In 1649, Queen Christina of Sweden persuaded Descartes to go to Stockholm. At her request, Descartes instructed the Queen in a series of early morning lessons. However, it's suggested that Descartes' custom of remaining in bed until nearly noon meant that being forced to rise so early led to his immune system becoming suppressed, causing pneumonia. After spending only four months in Stockholm, Descartes died on February 11, 1650.

Other Works

- **MEDITATIONS ON FIRST PHILOSOPHY**
  Expands on the work in Discourse on Method regarding the mind and body, truth and error, and existence.
- **PRINCIPLES OF PHILOSOPHY**
  In this work Descartes tries to present the universe from a mathematical standpoint.
- **PASSIONS OF THE SOUL**
  This work, which was dedicated to Princess Elizabeth of Bohemia, deals with emotions.

GRAPHING LINES

Graph paper links the geometry of a function, in this case a line, with the algebra behind it, and it was Descartes, who we've just met, who was the first to make this connection. In short, a graph gives you a picture of an equation, a way to see what the numbers mean. The most common mathematical relationships are linear; for example, phone charges and minutes spent calling, or distance traveled at a constant speed over time. With so many applications, there is a great emphasis on linear functions, and there are many forms a linear function can take, many different equations to represent a line. Here are three commonly used forms.

Slope-Point Form

For this first example we will give the information about the line, then find the equation and graph the line. The equation in slope-point form is: $y - y_1 = m(x - x_1)$, where x_1 and y_1 represent the point on the line and m represents the slope of the line.

To help, let's do an example. A line passes through the point (3, 4) and has a slope of $\frac{2}{3}$. Write the equation and graph the line.

Well, (3, 4) is the point and in the formula is represented by x_1 and y_1, while m represents the slope $\frac{2}{3}$. So the equation is $y - 4 = \frac{2}{3}(x - 3)$.

To graph the line we go to the point on the graph paper and plot it. Next, $\frac{2}{3}$ is the slope which represents the rise and run of the line therefore $\frac{2}{3} = \frac{\text{rise}}{\text{run}}$.

From the point (3, 4) we rise two units and run right three units. Lastly, we draw a line through the points to complete the graph below.

GRAPH 12

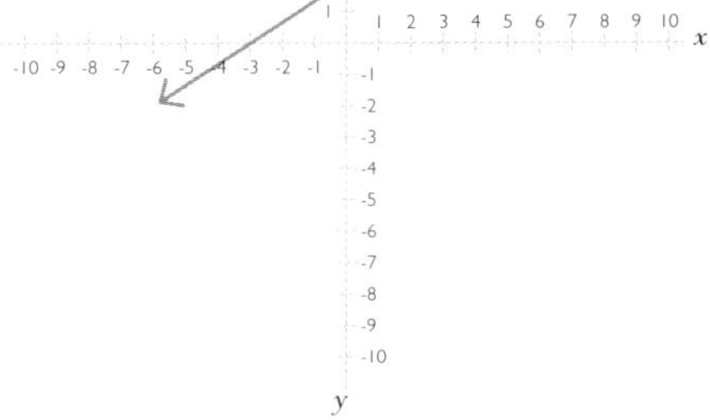

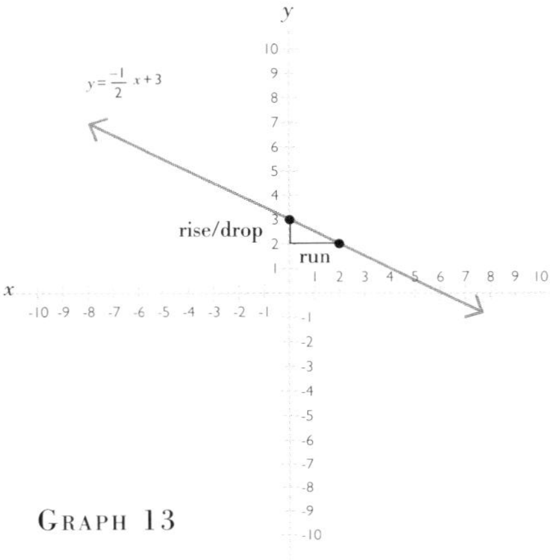

GRAPH 13

GRAPH 14

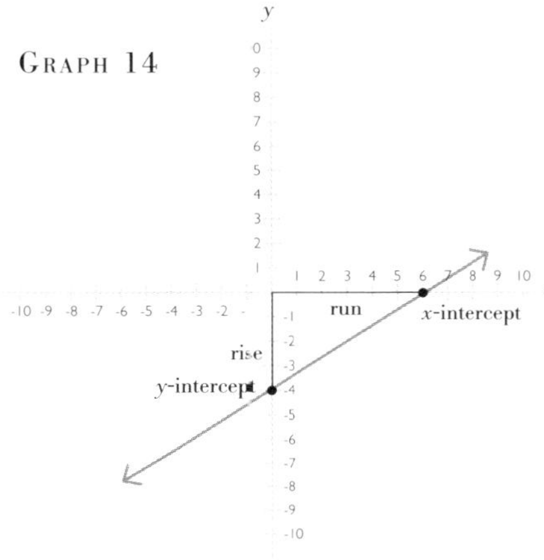

Slope y-Intercept Form

In this second example we have a graph of the line, and have to find the equation and information for the line. The equation in slope y-intercept form looks like $y = mx + b$, where m is the slope and b is the y-intercept (in other words, where the graph crosses the y-axis). Let's find the slope and y-intercept of graph 13 then write the equation.

From the graph we see that the line crosses the y-axis at the point 3. This represents the y-intercept or b. From the y-intercept we see that the line drops one unit then moves right two units. This represents a slope of $\frac{-1}{2}$, therefore $m = \frac{-1}{2}$. Given this information the equation will look like: $y = \frac{-1}{2}x + 3$.

Standard Form

In this example, we have the equation and from it can graph the line and determine the information about it. An equation in standard form looks like $Ax + By = C$ where A, B, and C are integers and A must be positive. (The restrictions on A, B, and C are arbitrary.) As an example, let's graph $2x - 3y = 12$.

To graph this line let's use what I call the "cover up" method. The x and y axes are often overlooked, but when you have a point on the y-axis, you know one thing for sure, the x value of that point. The x value of any point on the y-axis is zero. This is very helpful. If we make $x = 0$ in the equation we will find a point on the y-axis. So we "cover up" the x term and solve the equation $-3y = 12$. By isolating y we get $y = -4$ which is the y-intercept.

We use the same approach to find the x-intercept: "cover up" the y term and get the equation $2x = 12$ or $x = 6$, which is the x-intercept.

We now have two points for graph 14 and can draw a line through them. Now that we have the line we can state information about it. We already know the x and y intercepts and from them we can find the slope of $\frac{4}{6}$ or $\frac{2}{3}$.

Exercise

15 Profit Optimization

THE PROBLEM:

Wayne makes hockey sticks and croquet mallets. Each involves a two-step process: machining and finishing. The machining time for a hockey stick is forty minutes and that for a mallet is twenty. The finishing time for a stick is fifteen minutes and for a mallet is thirty. There are up to forty hours per week available for machining, and thirty for finishing. The profit from a hockey stick is $50 and that from a croquet mallet is $35. How many hockey sticks and croquet mallets should Wayne make each week to maximize profit?

THE METHOD:

To solve an optimization problem like this we use a process called "linear programming."

Step 1. Set up equations to represent each aspect of the problem. For machining time the equation will look like $\frac{2}{3}H + \frac{1}{3}C \leq 40$. Reading this equation we get $\frac{2}{3}$ of an hour spent machining each hockey stick plus $\frac{1}{3}$ of an hour spent machining each croquet mallet; in total these must be less than or equal to 40 hours.

For the finishing time the equation will look like $\frac{1}{4}H + \frac{1}{2}C \leq 30$. Reading the equation we get $\frac{1}{4}$ of an hour spent finishing each hockey stick plus $\frac{1}{2}$ an hour spent finishing each croquet mallet; in total these must be less than or equal to 30 hours.

For profit, the equation looks like this: $profit = 50H + 35C$ (profit equals $50 for each hockey stick and $35 for each croquet mallet).

Step 2. In preparation to graph the equations for machining and finishing both need to be in standard form. These equations are almost there, but unfortunately have fractions. However, if we multiplied every term in the machining equation ($\frac{2}{3}H + \frac{1}{3}C \leq 40$) by three we can get rid of the fractions. Remember that we should multiply both sides of the equation so that we don't change the solution. This gives $2H + 1C \leq 120$.

Now, if we multiply every term in the finishing equation ($\frac{1}{4}H + \frac{1}{2}C \leq 30$) by four we get $1H + 2C \leq 120$.

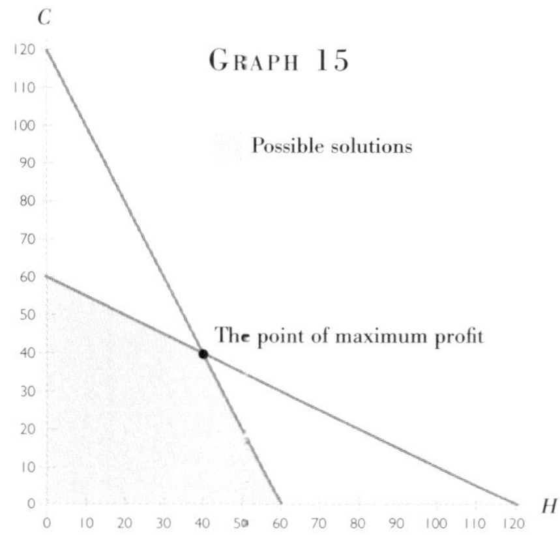

Step 3. Next we graph the equations using the "cover up" method.

$2H + 1C \leq 120$ has an H-intercept of 60 (I'm making the x-axis the hockey-stick axis) and a C-intercept (the y-axis) of 120. So $1H + 2C \leq 120$ has an H-intercept of 120 and a C-intercept of 60.

When we graph these lines we create an area of acceptable values for H and C. The only acceptable values of H and C are on or below these two lines. Also, acceptable values will only be above the H-axis and right of the C-axis because we're not making negative numbers of hockey sticks or croquet mallets. This then forms a quadrilateral (a four-sided shape) where all the acceptable values can be found.

If you try a point outside this region you will find that it will fail one or both of the equations. For example, let's take the point (70, 10). The machining equation ($2H + 1C \leq 120$) becomes $2(70) + 1(10) \leq 120$, or $140 + 10 \leq 120$ and $150 \leq 120$, which is incorrect, although it does pass the finishing equation.

If you try a point inside the quadrilateral you'll find that it works. As an example, we'll use (20, 40). For the first equation we get $2(20) + 1(40) \leq 120$, which becomes $80 \leq 120$, and for the second equation we get $1(20) + 2(40) \leq 120$, which becomes $100 \leq 120$. This is true for both points and therefore possible.

Step 4. The points of maximum and minimum profit are found at the vertices (corners) of the quadrilateral. From the graph we see these are at (0, 0), (0, 60), (60, 0), and (40, 40). We use these points in the equation ($profit = 50H + 35C$) to find which produces the most profit.

THE SOLUTION:

The highest value given when these four values are plugged into the profit equation is $50(40) + 35(40) = \$3400$. Wayne should make forty hockey sticks and forty croquet mallets each week to maximize his profit.

Profile

Blaise Pascal

Unlike Descartes, Pascal does not have a town named after him—although there is a street in Paris, and I'm sure many elsewhere, named in his honor. However, he can at least boast of having a unit of measurement named after him—the "pascal" (Pa) is used to measure pressure.

Blaise Pascal was born in Clermont (now Clermont-Ferrand), France in 1623. His father was Etienne Pascal, a mathematician and scientist in his own right. When Pascal was only three, tragedy struck and his mother died. His father never remarried. In 1632, Pascal's family moved to Paris.

Etienne educated his children himself. He wanted Pascal to have a firm grasp of languages so he forbade him from studying mathematics. This, however, only served to pique the young Pascal's curiosity, so he took it upon himself to study mathematics, developing the theorem for angles in a triangle. When Etienne saw this he relented and gave Pascal a copy of Euclid's *Elements* (see pages 54–5).

While in Paris, Etienne attended meetings of many of the great mathematical minds of France. These meetings were held by a monk, Marin Mersenne, who was also a friend of Descartes (see pages 116–17).

It was at one of these meetings held by Mersenne that Blaise Pascal, still a teenager, handed in his first work on mathematics, *Essay on Conic Sections*, published in 1640.

In his early twenties Pascal developed a machine to help his father with his work. Etienne was a tax collector and had to compute many numbers—Pascal's "Pascaline" eased that burden.

Also around this time Pascal conducted a series of experiments on pressure, and he used the results of these to argue for the existence of a vacuum. However, when he published his *New Experiment Concerning Vacuums*, in 1647, it led to disputes with other scientists. In fact, Descartes, who we've already met, disagreed with Pascal so much that he wrote that Pascal "has too much vacuum in his head."

In 1653, Pascal wrote his *Treatise on the Equilibrium of Liquid*, in which he gave us what has since become known as "Pascal's law of pressure." The law states that if pressure is applied to a non-compressible fluid then the pressure is conveyed to all the fluid and the container. This is a very helpful idea, and it's something to be thankful for the next time you apply the brakes on your car and the pressure you exert via the brake fluid is transmitted equally to all four wheels.

In the same year Pascal also published *Treatise on the Arithmetical Triangle*; and

although Pascal was far from the first to study this triangle it now has his name attached to it and has become known as "Pascal's triangle" (see pages 130–1 and 134–5).

Pascal and Faith

In 1651, when Pascal was twenty-eight, his father died, and Pascal wrote a letter to his sister outlining his thoughts on death. Then, in 1654, Pascal himself was involved in a serious accident. This brush with death was a turning point in his life, and Pascal pledged his life to Christianity. He began collecting his thoughts on the Christian faith in a work known simply as *Pensées* (*Thoughts*). The work was left incomplete when Pascal died in 1662; nevertheless it was published in 1670 and gave us one of the most interesting confluences of mathematics, philosophy, and religion, in the form of Pascal's "divine wager."

Rather than debate the existence of God, Pascal instead sets out a logical argument. He states there are four possible consequences to the combination of God's existence or non-existence and your belief or lack of it, as set out in the table below. In short, Pascal said that it's worth believing simply because you stand to lose nothing, but gain everything!

This does, however, leave many unanswered questions, among them is whether or not it is possible to base something as personal as faith on such a form of logic.

MERSENNE PRIMES

Marin Mersenne (1588–1648) gives his name to a set of primes. These follow the equation: $2^p - 1$, where p is a prime number. This equation does not work for all values of p, however, so it's not automatic that $2^p - 1$, is prime.

Mersenne primes are still being found today. In fact, you can join the Great Internet Mersenne Primes Search (GIMPS)—just download some software and the power of your computer is joined to others around the world. Mersenne primes are largely a curiosity, but large primes do have some applications in encryption. Here's a list of some early Mersenne primes:

The prime	Value of $2^p - 1$	Prime/ Not Prime
2	3	Prime
3	7	Prime
5	31	Prime
7	127	Prime
11	2047	Not Prime
13	8191	Prime
17	131071	Prime
19	524286	Prime

	God exists	God doesn't exist
You believe	You gain everything	You gain nothing
You don't believe	You gain nothing*	You gain nothing

*If God does exist, and He or She is vengeful, then this option could be worse than nothing!

FUN WITH FACTORIALS!

5!, what the heck does 5! mean? Does 5! mean that I'm really excited about the number five? Well, not quite. 5! is actually a factorial, which is effectively $5 \cdot 4 \cdot 3 \cdot 2 \cdot 1$. In spite of what you might believe, mathematics is about making your life easier. Multiplication is just a quick way to perform multiple additions, and a factorial (written as $n!$) is a quick way to multiply the natural numbers from one to n. Factorials are useful in all sorts of problems, as we'll find out later.

What Is a Factorial

The factorial function is defined as $n! = n(n - 1)(n - 2) \ldots (3)(2)(1)$. Or in plain English $n!$ is the natural numbers from n down to one multiplied together. For example, $5! = 5 \cdot 4 \cdot 3 \cdot 2 \cdot 1 = 120$. The one strange one is 0! which equals 1. Working with factorials is quite easy, and most cheap calculators have a factorial button.

Factorials are most often used in probability questions. As an example, you have five guys—Michael, Dean, Fred, Todd, and Roger—ready for a police line-up. How many ways can the five men be ordered? To answer this you could try and write out all of the options, but that's unreliable and time consuming. Mathematics is much quicker!

As the police officer sends them in she has choices to make. At first she has five choices—any of the men. For the second person she now has four choices (because one has already gone in). For the third person she has three choices, then two, then one.

So the number of ways she can arrange the usual suspects in a police line-up is 5!, or $5 \cdot 4 \cdot 3 \cdot 2 \cdot 1$, or 120.

Working With Factorials

Factorials are fun to work with, mostly because they make you look smart. For example, you might think simplifying $\frac{10!}{9!}$ would be tricky, but the answer is simply 10. I don't even need a calculator to tell you this, because the definition of a factorial pretty much makes the problem go away. Here's a different way of writing the factorial:

$$\frac{10!}{9!} = \frac{10 \cdot 9 \cdot 8 \cdot 7 \cdot 6 \cdot 5 \cdot 4 \cdot 3 \cdot 2 \cdot 1}{9 \cdot 8 \cdot 7 \cdot 6 \cdot 5 \cdot 4 \cdot 3 \cdot 2 \cdot 1}$$

This doesn't look nice, but you can see that most of the numbers in the numerator and denominator can cancel each other out:

$$\frac{10!}{9!} = \frac{10 \cdot \cancel{9} \cdot \cancel{8} \cdot \cancel{7} \cdot \cancel{6} \cdot \cancel{5} \cdot \cancel{4} \cdot \cancel{3} \cdot \cancel{2} \cdot \cancel{1}}{\cancel{9} \cdot \cancel{8} \cdot \cancel{7} \cdot \cancel{6} \cdot \cancel{5} \cdot \cancel{4} \cdot \cancel{3} \cdot \cancel{2} \cdot \cancel{1}} = 10$$

This approach can be very helpful. For example, if we had $\frac{8!}{6!}$ we could reduce it to $\frac{8 \cdot 7 \cdot 6!}{6!}$ where the 6! on the top and bottom would cancel, leaving $8 \cdot 7 = 56$.

I call this "peeling the onion," and it's a great way to imagine working with factorials. Using the above example, the 8! is an onion with eight layers to it while the 6! has six layers. To cancel out the onions you must make them the same size.

So the 8! onion needs to have two layers removed, the eighth layer and the seventh layer. Now in the numerator you have two layers of onion (eight and seven) and an onion with six layers. Now the six-layer onion in the numerator can cancel with the six-layer onion in the denominator.

This is helpful when confronted by a problem like $\frac{100!}{98!}$. This problem cannot be done on a calculator. Just try it; the 100! is too large for a calculator to cope with. Luckily we humans have a brain, so let's use it to peel the onion:

$$\frac{100!}{98!} = \frac{100 \cdot 99 \cdot 98!}{98!} = 100 \cdot 99 = 9900$$

There, nice and easy and it makes you look smart!

Turn to pages 136–7 to see how factorials are applied to binomials.

Now for one last example of onion peeling:

$$\frac{16!}{14! \cdot 5!}$$

To simplify, let's peel the 16! until it looks like a 14!:

$$\frac{16 \cdot 15 \cdot 14!}{14! \cdot 5!}$$

Now we cancel out the 14! above and below the line:

$$\frac{16 \cdot 15}{5!}$$

We can now write out the 5! as a collection of multiplications:

$$\frac{16 \cdot 15}{5 \cdot 4 \cdot 3 \cdot 2 \cdot 1}$$

Basic arithmetic tells us that 5 and 3 can multiply together to give 15, so we can remove them along with the 15 in the numerator to leave:

$$\frac{16}{4 \cdot 2 \cdot 1}$$

Multiply the numbers in the denominator together to give:

$$\frac{16}{8} \text{ or } 2$$

All this work without a calculator. Feel the power of factorials flow through you!

PERMUTATIONS AND COMBINATIONS

Every January at the school where I teach, students return from two weeks of fun in the snow. Once back in our hallways, there are always a few who forget the combination for their lockers. The funny thing is that what they have forgotten is not a combination; it's really a permutation, and all those locks should really be called permutation locks. Want to know why? Read on.

Permutations

A permutation is defined as the number of ways to obtain an ordered subset of r elements from a set of n elements. An example will clear up the jargon.

In the Olympic 100-meters final there are eight people. How many different ways can these eight people stand on the podium (first, second, and third)?

Since we're only looking to put three of the eight people on the podium, these three people are the subset r, while all eight people are represented by n. The fact we're placing them in first, second, and third positions means that they have an order. Therefore we have an ordered subset of three people from a set of eight people.

The notation for permutations looks like ${}_nP_r$ or $P(n, r)$ where n is the total number of objects and r is the number of arranged objects. In fact, most cheap scientific calculators have an ${}_nP_r$ button.

The formula that we should use to find our answer is:

$$ {}_nP_r = \frac{n!}{(n-r)!} $$

For the above example we would have:

$$ \frac{8!}{(8-3)!} = \frac{8!}{5!} = \frac{8 \cdot 7 \cdot 6 \cdot 5!}{5!} = 8 \cdot 7 \cdot 6 = 336 $$

Now the calculator can do this for you, but I find a certain amount of satisfaction in doing calculations myself.

Another way to look at this problem is to approach it like the police line-up on page 124. How many choices do we have for the winning runner? Any of the runners could win, so we have eight. For the second-place runner we have seven choices (because one has already crossed the line) and for the third-place runner we have six. Multiplying these together gives us the same answer, 336.

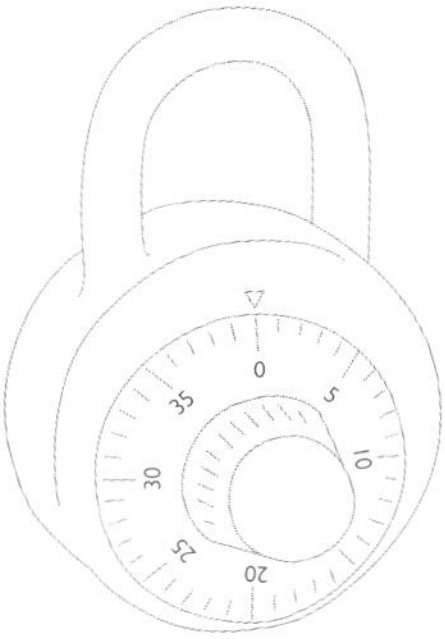

Combinations

A combination is very similar to a permutation, but there is one significant difference. Whereas a permutation is the number of ways to obtain an ordered subset of r elements from a set of n elements, a combination is the number of ways to obtain an unordered subset of r elements from a set of n elements. The notation for combination is ${}_nC_r$ or $\binom{n}{r}$. The formula we use is:

$${}_nC_r = \frac{n!}{(n-r)!r!}$$

To demonstrate the difference between permutations and combinations let's modify the above question. In the qualifying heats for the Olympic hundred meters, the first three across the line advance to the next round.

From a field of eight competitors, how many ways can three competitors advance? Because all you need to do to advance is finish in the top three, it no longer matters if you're first, second, or third. This makes the subset r an unordered subset. To calculate we get:

$${}_nC_r = \frac{8!}{(8-3)!3!} = \frac{8!}{5! \cdot 3!} = \frac{8 \cdot 7 \cdot 6 \cdot 5!}{5! \cdot 3!} = \frac{8 \cdot 7 \cdot 6}{3 \cdot 2 \cdot 1} = 56$$

This means that while there were 336 different permutations for who came home with the medals from the final, there are just 56 combinations for the different athletes that can make it through the qualifying heats.

The sharp-eyed among you might have noticed that the number of combinations is less than the number of permutations. The value of a combination will always be less than or equal to the value of the permutation; in fact, there's a formula for the relationship between permutations and combinations, which is:

$${}_nC_r = \frac{{}_nP_r}{r!}$$

To Order or Not to Order?

Often people forget which function to use when the order is important and when the order is unimportant. I just use a simple mnemonic to remind myself: **p**ermutations are **p**icky about **p**osition, while **c**ombinations **c**ouldn't **c**are less. There's nothing like a bit of alliteration to make something stick in the old gray cells.

Now let's go back to our school lockers. Why should our combination locks really be called permutation locks? Well, a lock requires the student to input a few numbers in a certain order, let's say three numbers. A lock that is set to 33, 21, 45 will not open if you input 21, 33, 45. Therefore the order is important and that lock should really be called a permutation lock.

Exercise 16

David, Stephen, Graham, and Neil

THE PROBLEM:

David, Stephen, Graham, and Neil are going out on a reunion tour. In the past there have been some ego issues, so on this tour they want to make sure that each performer gets equal billing when they walk out on stage. To make it fair, they want to make sure that the order in which they walk out will cover all options. In how many different orders can David, Stephen, Graham, and Neil walk out on stage?

THE METHOD:

One approach is to write out all the possible configurations:

David, Stephen, Graham, Neil

David, Stephen, Neil, Graham

David, Graham, Stephen, Neil

David, Graham, Neil, Stephen

David, Neil, Stephen, Graham

David, Neil, Graham, Stephen

… and so on.

But let's face it, this gets old pretty quickly and there's no guarantee that you wouldn't miss out one of the options. So far we have only done those with David first and we already have six different orders. (There are, in fact, six orders each for Stephen, Graham, and Neil, giving a total of twenty-four.)

A second approach is to use the "fundamental principle of counting." For something with such a fancy name, it's really quite simple. If you have n ways to pick one item and m ways to pick another, then you have $n \cdot m$ ways to pick both. As an example, if you have five shirts and three ties you can have fifteen shirt-tie combos ($5 \cdot 3 = 15$). I'm not saying they'd all look good, though.

We can apply the same principle to the four guys in the band. There are four options for which person will walk out first. We then have three options for the person who walks out second (one less because someone is already on stage). Then we have two choices for the third person, and one choice for the last. This gives us $4 \cdot 3 \cdot 2 \cdot 1 = 24$.

One last approach is to use permutations (see pages 126–7). For this example we have to arrange four people from a group of four or:

$$_4P_4 = \frac{4!}{(4-4)!}$$

Turn to pages 126–7 for more information on permutations.

Well, on the bottom we do the (4–4) giving 0!, which we know from earlier is really 1 in disguise, and we can separate out the factorial on top to give:

$$_4P_4 = \frac{4 \cdot 3 \cdot 2 \cdot 1}{1} \text{ or } \frac{24}{1}$$

So the answer is simply 24.

THE SOLUTION:

David, Stephen, Graham, and Neil can walk out on stage in twenty-four different ways. Let's hope the number of tour dates is a multiple of that.

• It'll be the twenty-fifth show before you see David, Stephen, Graham, and Neil lining up in the same way twice. All of the permutations are listed below.

1,2,3,4 3,1,2,4
1,2,4,3 3,1,4,2
1,3,2,4 3,2,1,4
1,3,4,2 3,2,4,1
1,4,2,3 3,4,1,2
1,4,3,2 3,4,2,1
2,1,3,4 4,1,2,3
2,1,4,3 4,1,3,2
2,3,1,4 4,2,1,3
2,3,4,1 4,2,3,1
2,4,1,3 4,3,1,2
2,4,3,1 4,3,2,1

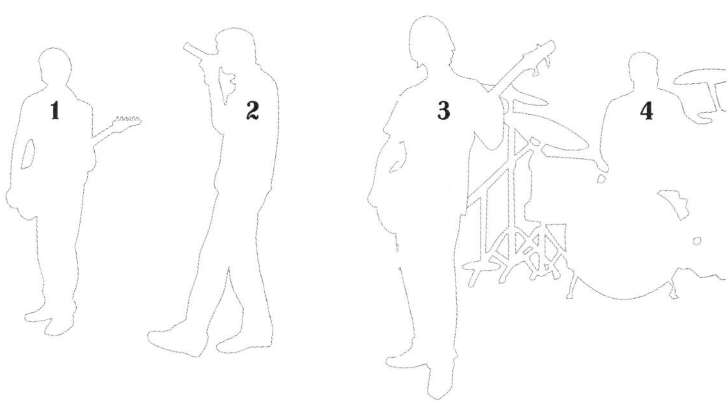

PASCAL'S TRIANGLE **Part I**

Pascal's triangle is full of mathematical goodness—a cornucopia of cool calculations is contained within. But first it should be pointed out that Pascal was not the first mathematician to discover this triangle. References to what we call Pascal's triangle can be found in Chinese, Indian, and Persian mathematics well before the birth of Pascal. It's just the Western bias we've seen before that attaches his name to it.

Making Pascal's Triangle

Pascal's triangle goes back a long way. Its connection to the expansion of binomials (see pages 34–5) made it very useful in early mathematics, and early references to something almost exactly like it can be found as early as the work of sixth-century Indian mathematician Varahamhira. Then, in tenth-century Persia, Al-Karaji worked with Pascal's triangle. Chinese mathematicians made reference to it as far back as the eleventh century, when Jia Xian gave Pascal's triangle to seven rows. Even in Europe, Petrus Apianus, a sixteenth-century German, used Pascal's triangle on the title page of a book on arithmetic.

Constructing Pascal's triangle is simple. You start with one at the apex then diagonally below it you write two more ones. As you descend through the rows, the ones continue along the left and right diagonals, and the numbers inside the triangle are found by adding the two numbers that are immediately above left and above right.

Patterns in Pascal's Triangle

Inside Pascal's triangle is a wonder of mathematical patterns. The first left and right diagonals all contain the number one. In the second diagonals you can find the natural number set; the third diagonals contain triangular numbers, and every second number in the third diagonal is a hexagonal number; while the fourth diagonals contain tetrahedral numbers. There are patterns of other exotic-sounding numbers such as pentatopes (strange four-dimensional tetrahedrons) and Catalan numbers, but unfortunately we don't have space for them here.

• Building Pascal's triangle is quite straightforward.

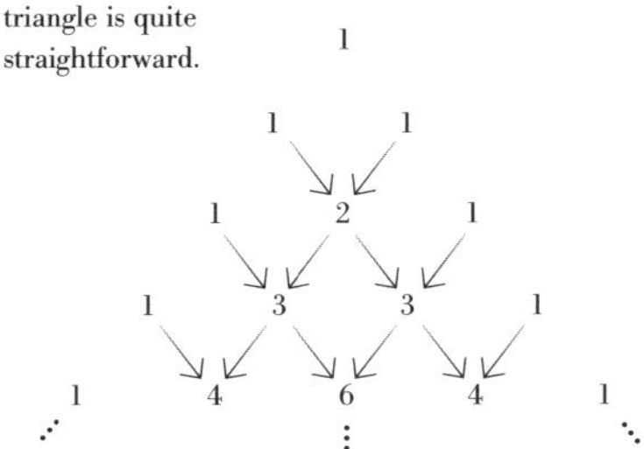

Powers in Pascal's Triangle

Another interesting bit of mathematics hidden in Pascal's triangle can be found if you sum the numbers of its rows. The sum of the first row is one; the second row gives two; and the third row gives four. The fourth row sums to eight, the fifth gives sixteen, and so on. You may have noticed that the sum of the digits in each row of Pascal's triangle is a power of two (see box right).

Row in Pascal's Triangle	Sum of Numbers	Power of two
1	1	2^0
2	2	2^1
3	4	2^2
4	8	2^3
5	16	2^4
6	32	2^5

Along with powers of two, Pascal's triangle also contains powers of eleven. If you look at the first row, you have the number one. This is 11^0 (anything to the power zero is one). The second row can be read as 11, which is 11^1, while the next row can be viewed as 121 or 11^2. From this start it's easy to guess the value of 11^3, it's 1331; and following that 11^4 is 14641.

At this point it gets a little more complicated: 11^5 is 161051—not the numbers of the fifth row of Pascal's triangle. The reason for this is we are now faced with two-digit numbers.

However, we can still make the pattern work because the digits in the triangle represent powers of ten. Starting from the right we have the units, then the tens, hundreds, thousands, and so on. In the fifth row the hundreds and thousands spots both have a 10 in them. This means we have to carry forward the hundreds to the thousands column, and the thousands to the tens-of-thousands column.

Let's take a closer look. The numbers of the fifth row, where we should find 11^5, are 1, 5, 10, 10, 5, 1. The 1 on the right represents the units, the 5 is in the tens column, and so on. This can be shown as:

fifth row:	1	5	10	10	5	1
1s						1
10s					5	0
100s				10	0	0
1000s			10	0	0	0
10,000s		5	0	0	0	0
100,000s	1	0	0	0	0	0

Carrying over the 10s in the hundreds and thousands columns gives 0 in the hundreds column. 1 in the thousands column, and 6 in the tens of thousands column. So:

$11^5 =$ 1 6 1 0 5 1

Therefore, with a little carrying forward you have all the powers of eleven, and this is just the start of the math-magic of Pascal's triangle. There's far more fun stuff that can be found on pages 134–5.

Exercise 17 The Handshake Problem

THE PROBLEM:

Bob and Bono are planning to have a big party. They plan on having twenty people at the party, excluding themselves. They want to make sure that each person gets a chance to meet every other person—they all know Bob and Bono, but none of them know each other—so they hire a professional introducer to make the introductions. The introducer charges $2 an introduction and spends a minute and fifteen seconds on each introduction before moving on to another pair. How many introductions does he make? How much money does he get; and how much does he earn an hour?

THE METHOD:

One method for solving this problem is to make a systematic list of all the introductions. This would be a large list of introductions for twenty but if we use a smaller set, a pattern may develop. Let's use six people.

A meets B; B meets C; C meets D; D meets E; E meets F

A meets C; B meets D; C meets E; D meets F

A meets D; B meets E; C meets F

A meets E; B meets F

A meets F

The number of introductions decreases by one each time because we don't have to repeat introductions already made. (That's to say once Andy has been introduced to Bruce, then Bruce does not need to be reintroduced to Andy.) So with six people, we would have $1 + 2 + 3 + 4 + 5 = 15$ introductions. (By the way, fifteen is the fifth triangular number; see pages 16–17.)

For twenty guests, Andy would be introduced to nineteen people, then Bruce would have eighteen introductions, Chris seventeen and so on. The number of introductions would be $19 + 18 + 17 + 16 + 15 + 14 + 13 + 11 + 10 + 9 + 8 + 7 + 6 + 5 + 4 + 3 + 2 + 1 = 190$. That's a heck of a long sum, but it turns out that it's also the nineteenth triangular number. As it happens, we've a formula for finding triangular numbers:

$$\frac{(n)(n-1)}{2}$$

or for this example:

$$\frac{(20)(19)}{2} = 190$$

Turn to page 137 for using combinations to solve binomials.

Another approach is to use combinations, which we already met on page 127. As it doesn't matter whether Andy meets Bruce or Bruce meets Andy, the order is unimportant, so this is a combination rather than a permutation. As we saw before, a combination is the number of ways to select r elements from a set of n elements. In our case it's the number of ways to select two people from a group of twenty or:

$$_{20}C_2 = \frac{20!}{18! \cdot 2!} = \frac{20 \cdot 19 \cdot 18!}{18! \cdot 2!} = \frac{20 \cdot 19}{2} = 190$$

This represents the number of handshakes. If the professional introducer gets \$2 per introduction he makes $190 \cdot \$2 = \$380$. If he takes one minute and 15 seconds or 1.25 minutes per introduction, the introducer will work for $190 \cdot 1.25 = 237.5$ minutes, or 3.9583 hours; or rounded up a little, four hours. This means he makes $380 \div 4 = \$95$ per hour.

THE SOLUTION:

The introducer makes 190 introductions. He makes \$380 dollars at \$95 per hour.

If this kind of thing looks familiar it's because the answers to combination problems can be found in Pascal's triangle. In this case $_{20}C_2$ happens to be the third term in the twenty-first row.

PASCAL'S TRIANGLE **Part 2**

As we've already discovered, there is a sense of beauty and symmetry to Pascal's triangle; and like that of the Fibonacci sequence and the golden ratio, it's a beauty that requires no great understanding of higher mathematics.

The Beauty of Pascal's Triangle

To unlock the beauty in Pascal's triangle all you need is a set of crayons and a sense of adventure. Choose a set of numbers with something in common—for example, multiples of five—and color them in. Alternatively, pick any number and divide the numbers in Pascal's triangle by it, but leave remainders rather than using decimal places. The remainders will range from zero to one less than the number you chose—assign colors to different remainders and color in those spots. If you do either of the above you'll start to see some amazing patterns emerge; use your imagination and start searching for other patterns.

Using the previous approach to obtain remainders, but dividing by two and coloring a remainder of one while leaving a remainder of zero white, will form what is known as Sierpinski's triangle. The triangle is named after the Polish mathematician Waclaw Sierpinski (1882–1969), who described it in 1915. This shows that even in the modern era we are still making new connections to mathematics that has been known for centuries.

This is an example of the triangle's connection to fractal geometry (you know, the type of thing that shows up on those posters of weird spirals and patterns). A relatively new branch of mathematics, the term "fractal" was only coined in 1975 by French mathematician Benoit Mandelbrot.

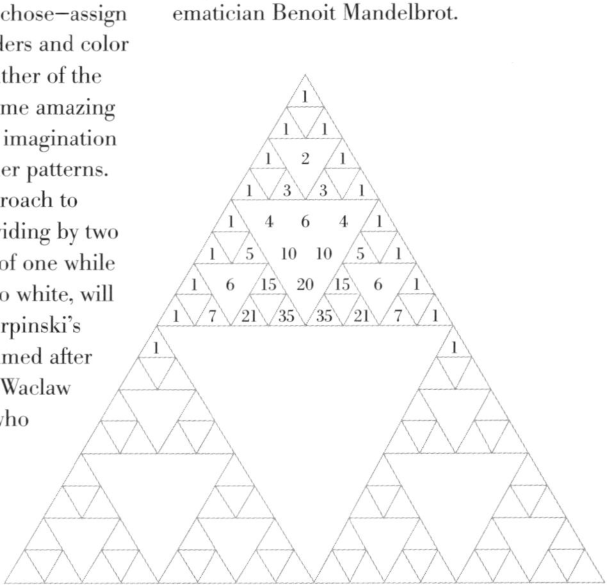

• Sierpinski's triangle—a fractal pattern that can be found within Pascal's triangle.

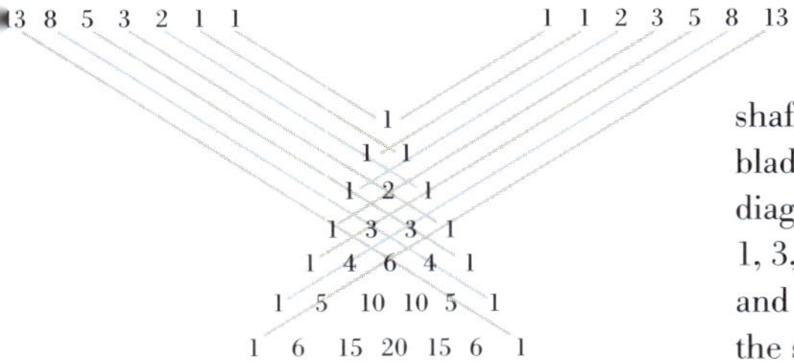

Pascal's Triangle and Fibonacci

Another neat trick is to take the shallow diagonals of the triangle and add the terms together (see above) to get the Fibonacci sequence. This connects three of the coolest things in mathematics: Pascal's triangle, the Fibonacci sequence, and the golden ratio.

Pascal's Hockey Sticks

For me, it's nice to see Canada's national sport reflected in Pascal's triangle. If you add the numbers in any diagonal you will find the sum of those numbers in the next row. For example, let's add a few of the terms in the fifth diagonal on the left. In this diagonal the numbers are 1, 5, 15, 35, 70, and so on. If we sum these we get 126—one row down and one spot to the left. So the numbers form the shaft and the sum forms the stick's blade. On the right let's look at the third diagonal and add the first four numbers: 1, 3, 6, 10. Their sum is one row down and one spot to the right. The shaft of the stick can be any length but must start with a 1; the blade of the stick is always one down and one to the left or right, depending on where you start.

Pascal's Triangle and flowers

One last neat property of Pascal's triangle is Pascal's petals. If you take any term, other than the ones on the edge, it will be surrounded by six other terms like the petals of a flower. If you multiply the three terms opposite each other you will find they have the same product as the other three terms. As an example, let's look at the term six rows down and three to the right. This has a value of 10. Around it we have the numbers 4, 6, 10, 20, 15, and 5. If we multiply the non-adjacent numbers 4, 10, and 15 we get 600. If we multiply the remaining non-adjacent numbers 6, 20, and 5 we get 600. Pretty neat, huh?

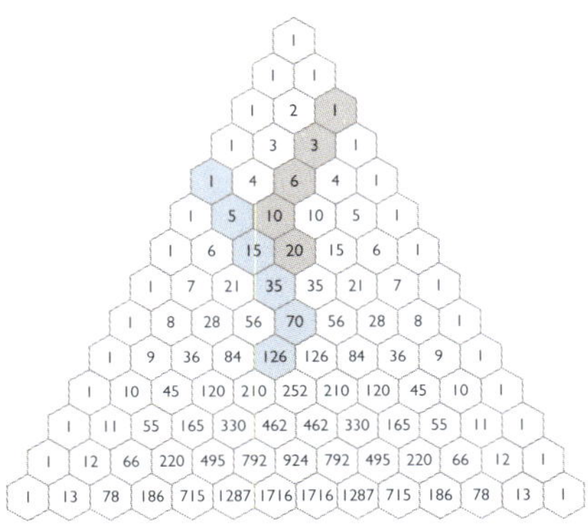

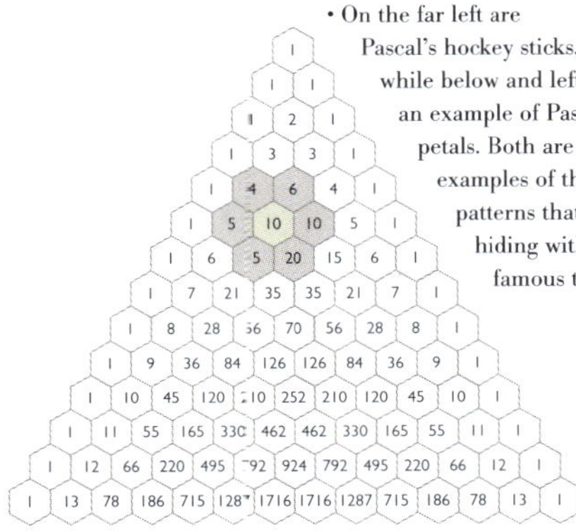

• On the far left are Pascal's hockey sticks, while below and left is an example of Pascal's petals. Both are great examples of the patterns that are hiding within this famous triangle.

THE BINOMIAL THEOREM

The binomial theorem is a nice simple way to expand (or multiply out) binomials. The biggest application of the binomial theorem is within probability problems in which there are only two choices, to you and me that's something like tossing a coin. This might seem limiting, but in reality it's very easy and useful to divide things into two groups.

Let's Expand Some Binomials

If we expand $(x + y)^0$ we get one, as anything to the zero power is one. If we expand $(x + y)^1$ we get $1x + 1y$.

Then if we expand $(x + y)^2$ we need to write it out twice $(x + y)(x + y)$ and "foil" (see pages 34–5). This gives $1x^2 + 1xy + 1xy + 1y^2$, which when you collect like terms is $1x^2 + 2xy + 1y^2$.

If we expand $(x + y)^3$, we need to write it out three times as:

$$(x + y)(x + y)(x + y)$$

Next we "foil" out the first two binomials and simplify. This gives:

$$(x^2 + 2xy + 1y^2)(x + y)$$

Then the trinomial and the binomial need to be multiplied, giving:

$$1x^3 + 1x^2y + 2x^2y + 2xy^2 + 1xy^2 + 1y^3$$

After this we need to collect like terms to give:

$$1x^3 + 3x^2y + 3xy^2 + 1y^3$$

As you can imagine, this gets old very quickly. I love mathematics, but even I don't feel like writing out the next expansion, so I won't. Luckily there's a nicer way to deal with binomial expansions. Here's what we have so far:

$$(x + y)^0 = 1$$
$$(x + y)^1 = 1x + 1y$$
$$(x + y)^2 = 1x^2 + 2xy + 1y^2$$
$$(x + y)^3 = 1x^3 + 3x^2y + 3xy^2 + 1y^3$$

If we look at the coefficients of the expansions we see they are numbers from Pascal's triangle. If we wanted to expand the binomial $(x + y)^4$ we could do it without all the mess presented above. Here's $(x + y)^4$ expanded:

$$(x + y)^4 = 1x^4 + 4x^3y + 6x^2y^2 + 4xy^3 + 1y^4$$

Now the coefficients are just one aspect of the expansion, another is the variables. If you look at the last expansion, the x variable starts with an exponent of four and decreases until the x variable disappears on the last term. (In fact, it's there but is x^0, which as we've said before is equal to one.)

So the exponents on x go: four, three, two, one, and zero. The y variable starts with an exponent of zero and rises to an exponent of four. Also, the sum of exponents on any term in this expansion is four. The focus on four is due to the exponent of the original binomial, which is $(x + y)^4$. So if we wanted to expand $(x + y)^5$, we could just follow Pascal's triangle and add in the variables:

Turn to pages 126–7 for more information on combinations.

$$(x + y)^5 = 1x^5 + 5x^4y + 10x^3y^2 + 10x^2y^3 + 5xy^4 + 1y^5$$

Let's Expand with Factorials

What happens if you are asked to expand $(x + y)^{13}$? Do you really want to write out fourteen rows of Pascal's triangle just to get the coefficients to the expansion? No! Luckily you can use factorials to find the coefficients of the expansion. Looking at the last example:

$$1x^5 + 5x^4y + 10x^3y^2 + 10x^2y^3 + 5xy^4 + 1y^5$$

The coefficient of the second term is five. This number can be found by writing a factorial statement. The sum of exponents on x and y is five, x has an exponent of four, and y has an exponent of one. We can write this as $\frac{5!}{4!\cdot1!}$ which equals five. The next term has three for the x exponent and two for the y exponent. This can be written as $\frac{5!}{3!\cdot2!}$ which equals ten. So the coefficient is:

$$\frac{\text{(sum of exponents)!}}{\text{(first exponent)!(second exponent)!}}$$

Now, if we wanted to expand $(x + y)^{13}$—and why wouldn't we?—we could write out the variables first then add the coefficients later. The first five terms without coefficient would look like:

$$x^{13} + x^{12}y + x^{11}y^2 + \ldots$$

Adding the coefficients gives:

$$\frac{13!}{13!0!}x^{13} + \frac{13!}{12!1!}x^{12}y + \frac{13!}{11!2!}x^{11}y^2 + \ldots$$

Evaluating the factorials gives:

$$1x^{13} + 13x^{12}y + 78x^{11}y^2 + \ldots$$

Another Way to Expand

Another way to find the coefficients of a binomial expansion is to use combinations. Using the last example of $(x + y)^{13}$ we could expand the first few terms as:

$${}_{13}C_0x^{13} + {}_{13}C_1x^{12}y + {}_{13}C_2x^{11}y^2 + \ldots$$

All three methods are essentially the same, just use whatever suits you.

Exercise 18

The Coin Toss

THE PROBLEM:

Jimmy offers Robert a wager. Jimmy will flip a coin ten times. If a head shows up zero, one, two, three, seven, eight, nine, or ten times he will give Robert a dollar. If a head shows up four, five, or six times Robert must give Jimmy a dollar. Should Robert take the wager?

THE METHOD:

Most people feel that they have an intuitive sense for "odds" or "risk." But the truth is that most people are terrible at assessing probability. Evidence of this is the number of people who buy lottery tickets or think that they can "beat the house" in a casino.

At this point I should confess that I buy lottery tickets—oh, the mathematical shame!—but I buy them for the entertainment of the dream: What would I do with a million? Also, there's a way to beat the house in blackjack, but it requires card counting, possibly getting thrown out of the casino, and, depending on whether you believe the movies, having a few fingers broken for your trouble. Now back to the question. Many people would take the bet because they see themselves as having eight chances to win verses three of losing … but, perhaps surprisingly, they would be wrong.

One way to show this would be to perform the wager over and over again to get a sense of what options are more common. If you repeat the act of tossing a coin ten times and counting the heads over and over, you will get a bar chart that follows the shape of a bell curve (see opposite) with five heads being the highest point, the commonest outcome.

A quicker and more accurate approach is to use the binomial theorem (see pages 136–7). Flipping a coin gives only two options: heads or tails, and can be written as a binomial $(h + t)$. If we flip the coin ten times we get $(h + t)^{10}$, a bracket for each flip. If we expand the binomial then we get the following expression:

$$h^{10} + 10h^9t + 45h^8t^2 + 120h^7t^3 + 210h^6t^4 + 252h^5t^5$$

$$+ 210h^4t^6 + 120h^3t^7 + 45h^2t^8 + 10ht^9 + t^{10}$$

Now, the probability of a head is $\frac{1}{2}$ and the probability of a tail is $\frac{1}{2}$. Jimmy is hoping for four, five, or six heads. The probability of four heads and six tails will be the term in the binomial expansion with four *h*s and six *t*s or $210h^4t^6$. Because the probability of a head or tail is $\frac{1}{2}$ we can plug this in:

$$210\left(\frac{1}{2}\right)^4\left(\frac{1}{2}\right)^6 \text{ or } 0.205078125$$

For five heads and five tails we get $252h^5t^5$ which equals:

$$252\left(\frac{1}{2}\right)^5\left(\frac{1}{2}\right)^5 \text{ or } 0.24609375$$

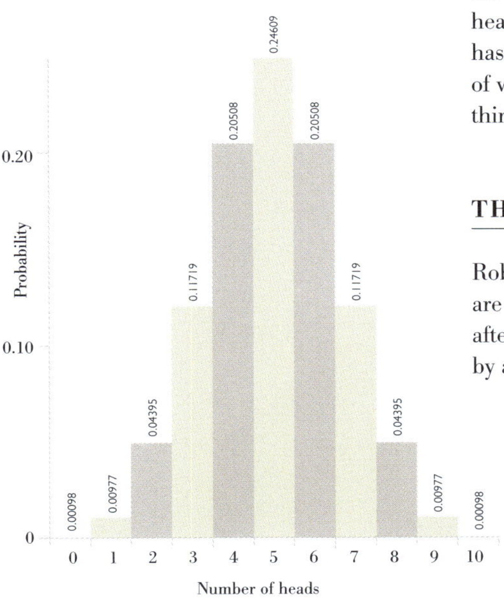

For six heads and four tails we get $210h^6t^4$ which equals

$$210\left(\frac{1}{2}\right)^6\left(\frac{1}{2}\right)^4 \text{ or } 0.205078125$$

If we add these amounts we find that the probability of getting four, five, or six heads is 0.65625 or 65.625%. Jimmy has an approximately two-thirds chance of winning while Robert only has a one third chance.

THE SOLUTION:

Robert should say no. The odds are stacked against him. On average, after three plays Jimmy would be up by a dollar.

Profile # Leonhard Euler

One of the most prolific mathematicians ever, Leonhard Euler, was born on April 15, 1707. His father Paul, an acquaintance of the famous Johann Bernoulli, had some mathematical training and taught his son elementary mathematics. Leonhard entered university in 1720 and his potential was soon discovered. On weekends Bernoulli would answer Leonhard's questions and suggest further reading for him. In 1723 Euler received a master's degree in philosophy. Although his father wanted him to study theology, Bernoulli helped Leonhard to convince his father to allow him to pursue mathematics.

St. Petersburg, Berlin, and Back

In 1726, when Nicolaus Bernoulli, Johann Bernoulli's eldest son, died Euler replaced him at the Imperial Russian Academy of Science, in St. Petersburg. Euler lived and worked with Bernoulli's second son, Daniel. However, Daniel became disenchanted with the Academy, and in 1733 he left, leaving Euler to replace him as senior chair of mathematics. In 1734 Euler married and eventually had thirteen children, only five of who survived infancy.

A change in the monarchy saw increasing tensions in St. Petersburg, so in 1741 Euler took a position in Berlin, where he would spend the next twenty-five years.

During that time he wrote many articles and in 1759 he assumed leadership of the Berlin Academy.

In 1766, Euler returned to the Imperial Russian Academy, but very soon afterwards he became blind. In spite of losing his sight, Euler continued to work with the help of his sons Johann and Christoph. In fact, Euler continued to publish until he passed away in St. Petersburg on September 18, 1783.

The Bridges of Konigsberg

The "Bridges of Konigsberg" is a classic problem. The town, then part of Prussia, but now Kalingrad in the little hunk of Russian territory between Lithuania and Poland, is on a river with two islands in it. There are seven bridges connecting the island to both sides of the river and to each other. The question was whether there was a way to start in one location and cross each bridge once and only once.

It's a strange task, to be sure, and one that Euler proved was impossible. The reason is based on the number of bridges to each land mass. For the land masses you don't start at or finish at, you must enter and leave. This requires two bridges, which means that any land mass that is not the start or finish point must have an even number of bridges. This is not the case for Konigsberg, where all four landmasses have an odd number of bridges. This leads to a thing called an "Eulerian path," which will allow you to cross

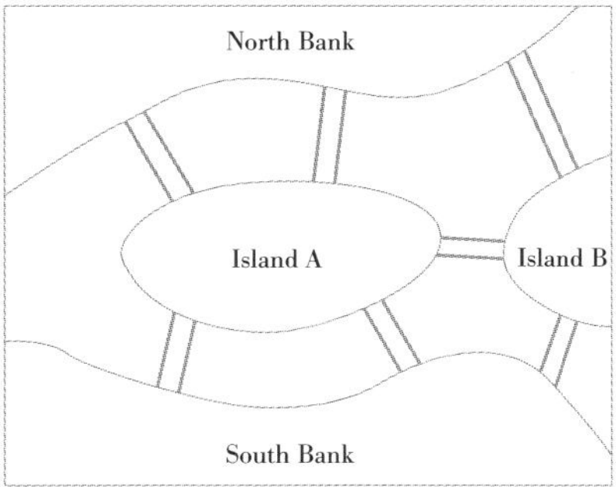

• The Bridges of Konigsberg can be reduced to nodes (land masses) and lines (bridges). Many maps follow this format; for example, train maps often just show the stations as nodes and the track as lines. Euler's path also has practical applications; for example, when haulage companies are looking to reduce fuel and travel costs and want to plan routes that do not involve doubling back on themselves.

each bridge (or edge) only once if and only if two of the land masses (or nodes) has an odd number of bridges. This would be possible if we removed the bridge between the two islands. An Eulerian cycle requires you to return to your starting point and it also requires that all of the land masses (nodes) should be attached to an even number of bridges (edges).

Related to the "Bridges of Konigsberg" question, Euler also gave us the formula $V - E + F = 2$ where the V is the number of vertices, E the number of edges, and F the number of faces of a polyhedron (see page 53).

A NOTE ON NOTATION

Euler is also responsible for producing some of the notations we use today. He gave us $f(x)$ for a function applied to a variable x, the Greek letter Σ (sigma) for summation, the letter i for imaginary numbers, and e for the value 2.71828... The first reference to e comes from a work published by John Napier (see page 160), but the discovery of the constant is credited to Jacob Bernoulli, the son of Euler's mentor. Euler started using the letter e for this constant and it stuck. The number e is another fabulous number like π and φ (see pages 18–19 and 100–1). The number e can be calculated using an infinite series as follows:

$$e = \frac{1}{0!} + \frac{1}{1!} + \frac{1}{2!} + \frac{1}{3!} + \frac{1}{4!} \ldots$$

This leads to one of the most beautiful equations in mathematics: $e^{i\pi} + 1 = 0$. I have thought of putting this on a T-shirt but I don't think people will like it as much as my π one.

Exercise 19

The Roads of Kantgetinshape

THE PROBLEM:

A middle-aged man stands contemplating life. Just after his forty-second birthday he looks down to see an expanding midriff. He decides he needs to start exercising again, but alas he is no longer twenty. Ah, to be twenty again: when you are twenty you run to get in shape; at thirty you run to stay in shape; at forty you run to slow the inevitable decline. Are you depressed yet? Michael wants to start a running program. A campground nearby is closed during the winters and would be a nice quiet place to run. The map of the campground is shown. Michael would like to start at the parking lot, run all the roads once, and end back in the parking lot. Can it be done? If not, how can he change things to make it work?

THE METHOD:

This is a classic Euler-cycle problem. Looking at the map, there are seven "nodes," or more simply seven places where roads meet. There are only two roads leading to and from the parking lot, so this is an even node. The other six nodes, however, are all odd. Therefore, in its present configuration there is no Euler cycle.

This means that Michael needs to compromise. Because the local ministry of the environment would get upset if he added a new road without asking nicely, all Michael can do is remove sections from his run, or maybe cover some sections twice. Let's label the sections of road. This gives us ten sections. Now let's label the nodes. In order to have an Euler cycle we need the number of sections joining each node to be even.

If we run a section twice it's like adding another road. Being enthusiastic about his fitness regime, Michael would like to remove short sections and double up on longer sections.

By running from *A* to *B* and then to *C*, Michael can remove road 2 and make *C* even. Then he can run from *C* to *D* and then to *E* and remove road 6, making *D* and *G* even. He can then run from *E* to *F* to *G* and back to *F*. If he runs over road section 9 again it's like adding another road and he makes *F* and *E* even. He can then run from *E* to *B*. Repeating the road section 1 again will make *B* and *A* even.

This will then be an Euler cycle. By the way, the route is 2.5 km (1.5 miles).

Turn to pages 140–1 for information on Euler cycles.

THE SOLUTION:

With the removal of two short sections and the repetition of two sections an Euler cycle can be made. The route would follow the road sections 1 → 3 → 4 → 5 → 9 → 7 → 8 → 9 → 10 → 1.

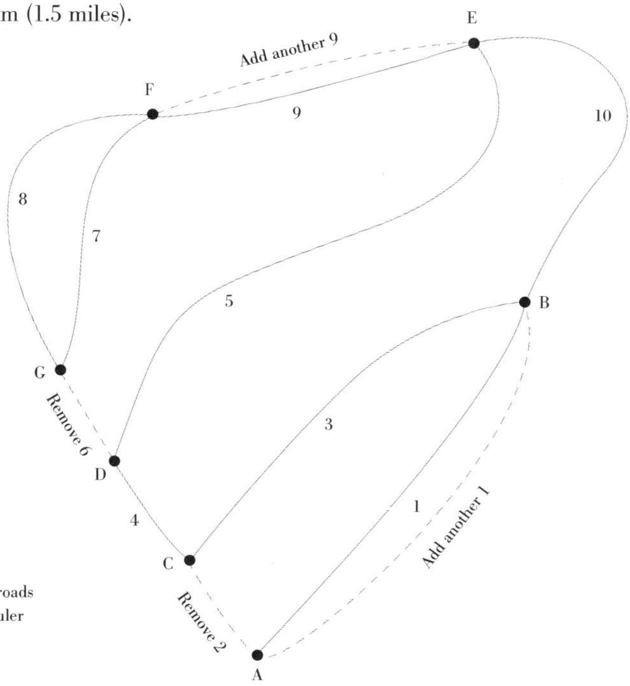

• Without adding or removing roads there would be no possible Euler cycle for these paths.

Profile

Carl Friedrich Gauss

Have you ever met someone who's a real know-it-all? When you tell them something you have just learned, they just reply: "Yeah, I knew that." Sometimes you believe them, but most of the time you think they're just full of it. Well, Carl Friedrich Gauss was that sort of guy, but he really did know it all. When we talk about freaky geniuses, Carl Friedrich Gauss is our best example.

Early Life

Gauss was born in Brunswick, Germany in 1777. At the age of seven, in elementary school he impressed his teacher with his brilliance (see pages 146–7). At the age of eleven he entered secondary school learning languages. In 1792, at fifteen, he entered Brunswick Collegium. When there Gauss independently discovered the binomial theorem (see page 136–7) among other mathematical concepts. Three years later Gauss left for Göttingen University. However, he left Göttingen without a degree and returned to Brunswick, receiving a degree in 1799. Gauss had been receiving a stipend from the Duke of Brunswick and, at his request, Gauss submitted a doctoral dissertation to the University of Helmstedt. Gauss's dissertation was on the fundamental theorem of algebra.

A Busy Few Years

Gauss married in 1805, but he could not have known what changes the next five years held in store for him. The Duke of Brunswick, Gauss's

Works

- **DISQUISITIONES ARITHMETICAE**
  Other than his dissertation, the Disquisitiones Arithmeticae, *in 1801, was Gauss's first published work. It dealt mostly with number theory which includes the study of primes (see pages 18–19) and Diophantine equations (see pages 66–7).*
- **THEORY OF CELESTIAL MOVEMENT**
  In 1809 Gauss published his second work. The book flowed naturally from his predictions of the paths of Ceres and Pallas—a dwarf planet and asteroid that were at the time thought to be new planets.
- **ARTICLES**
  Gauss also published many articles including papers on series, integration, statistics, and geometry.

THE FUNDAMENTALS OF ALGEBRA

One of Gauss's most important contributions to mathematics was his work into the "fundamental theorem of algebra." The theorem states that a polynomial with real or complex coefficients will have root(s) in the complex plane. Plainly stated, if you have a polynomial with a degree *n*, and the coefficients are real or complex numbers then you will have *n* roots or solutions. For example, on page 112 we looked at quadratics (parabolas) which had a degree of two and in all three cases there were two solutions—two unequal real solutions, two equal real solutions, and two complex solutions. Gauss produced a geometric proof of this in 1799, two further proofs in 1816, and a revision of his earlier proof in 1849.

supporter, died fighting the Prussians, and in 1807 Gauss took the position of director of the Göttingen Observatory. Previously Gauss had accurately predicted the position of two new celestial objects, Ceres (now classified as a dwarf planet) and Pallas (now classified as an asteroid). In 1808 Gauss's father died. Then, in 1809, Gauss's wife Johanna died during the birth of their second son, Louis, who only lived until 1810. A year later Gauss married Johanna's best friend Minna. In the years from 1805 to 1811, Gauss married twice (Johanna and Minna), fathered four children (Joseph, Wilhelmina, and Louis by Johanne and Eugene by Minna) and suffered three bereavements (the Duke, his wife Johanna, and son Louis). In anyone's book, that's a lot to deal with.

Later Years

In 1831 Gauss began to work with Wilhelm Weber (1804–91), a German physicist who had come to Göttingen at Gauss's request.

Together they produced many papers until Weber had to leave Göttingen in 1837 when the Hanoverian government objected to his political views.

Gauss died on February 23, 1855, but his work lives on in many forms. Two examples are that the SI unit of magnetic flux bears Weber's name; and the process of "degaussing," which removes the magnetic field from an object, is also named after Gauss. It's this action that makes the "thunk" sound when you switch your television or computer monitor on.

"It may be true that men who are mere mathematicians have certain specific shortcomings, but that is not the fault of mathematics, for it is equally true of every other exclusive occupation."

Exercise 20

Arithmetic Series

THE PROBLEM:

We're in late-eighteenth-century Germany. A tired and overworked teacher wants to get some work done, so he tells his class to add all the numbers from one to one hundred—that should keep them busy. But a snot-nosed pre-teen named Carl finishes the task in less than five minutes, and begins to bug the teacher. Though ticked off, the teacher recognizes the talent in this "prince of mathematics." Can you repeat Carl's trick?

THE METHOD:

Now Carl is no slouch. While the other children dive into the work adding the numbers from one to one hundred, Carl thinks first.

Carl could add the numbers from one to one hundred or he could add the numbers from one hundred to one, both would be the same result:

$$1+ 2 + 3 \ldots + 98 + 99 + 100 = sum$$

or

$$100 + 99 + 98 + \ldots. +3 +2 +1 = sum$$

Now after writing the list both forward and backward Carl notices that the sums of the columns are all the same, so adding top and bottom series will give twice the sum:

$$1 + 2 + 3 \ldots + 98 + 99 + 100 = sum$$

$$100 + 99 + 98 + \ldots + 3 + 2 + 1 = sum$$

$$101 + 101 + 101 \ldots + 101 + 101 + 101 = 2 \cdot sum$$

Carl then notices that he has a hundred 101s, so he can rewrite the series on the left as a multiplication:

$$100(101) = 2 \cdot sum$$

Dividing both sides by two to find the sum gives:

$$\frac{100(101)}{2} = sum$$

$$5050 = sum$$

THE SOLUTION:

The sum of the numbers from one to one hundred is 5050.

ARITHMETIC SERIES

The line of thinking shown by Gauss leads to a general formula from the sum of an arithmetic series.

First, an arithmetic series is a series where each number is found by adding a common number (common difference) to the previous number. One example of an arithmetic series is 3 + 7 + 11 + 15 + 19 + 23. In this series the first term is three, the common difference is four and the number of terms is six. The formula for the sum of an arithmetic series is

$$s = \frac{n}{2}(2a + (n - 1)d)$$

where a is the first term, d is the common difference and n is the number of terms. So, plugging in the numbers from the above series into the formula gives:

$$s = \frac{6}{2}(2 \cdot 3 + (6 - 1)4)$$

and this simplifies to $s = 3(6-(5)4)$, which when simplified further finally gives $s = 78$.

Exercise 21

Geometric Series

THE PROBLEM:

Bonnie is confronted with a terrible decision: She has won the lottery and must choose between two options. Option one is to take \$10,000,000 right now. Option two is to take 1¢ on the first day of a month, then 2¢ on the second day, 4¢ on the third day, and continue doubling like this until the end of the month. Which option should she take?

THE METHOD:

Both options are pretty good. I mean, who in their right mind would complain about \$10,000,000? The problem is that option two might provide more than \$10,000,000. Bonnie, though not a fan of mathematics, is willing to spend the time to find out which option is the best.

Option one = \$10,000,000

Option two = a little work

First, let's say that there are thirty days in this particular month. Now Bonnie can make a table of what she is given each day. You'll note from the table that we can write this in a few different ways.

Day	Money	Money (another way)	Money (a third way)
1	\$0.01	\$0.01	$\$0.01 \cdot 2^0$
2	\$0.02	$\$0.01 \cdot 2$	$\$0.01 \cdot 2^1$
3	\$0.04	$\$0.01 \cdot 2 \cdot 2$	$\$0.01 \cdot 2^2$
4	\$0.08	$\$0.01 \cdot 2 \cdot 2 \cdot 2$	$\$0.01 \cdot 2^3$
5	\$0.16	$\$0.01 \cdot 2 \cdot 2 \cdot 2 \cdot 2$	$\$0.01 \cdot 2^4$

Now this can be written as a sum:

$$sum = 0.01 \cdot 2^0 + 0.01 \cdot 2^1 + 0.01 \cdot 2^2 + 0.01 \cdot 2^3 + \ldots + 0.01 \cdot 2^{28} + 0.01 \cdot 2^{29}$$

This still requires adding thirty different numbers. Another approach is to use something similar to what Carl did with the arithmetic series (see pages 146–7). Bonnie takes the above series and multiplies it by two, giving:

$$2 \cdot sum = 0.01 \cdot 2^1 + 0.01 \cdot 2^2 + 0.01 \cdot 2^3 + 0.01 \cdot 2^4 + \ldots + 0.01 \cdot 2^{29} + 0.01 \cdot 2^{30}$$

Notice that multiplying by two has just added one to each exponent. (Bonnie chose two because it was the multiplier between terms thus making it easy to write.) Now we subtract the lesser series from the greater series:

$$\begin{aligned} 2 \cdot sum &= 0.01 \cdot 2^1 + 0.01 \cdot 2^2 + 0.01 \cdot 2^3 + \ldots + 0.01 \cdot 2^{28} + 0.01 \cdot 2^{29} + 0.01 \cdot 2^{30} \\ sum &= 0.01 \cdot 2^0 + 0.01 \cdot 2^1 + 0.01 \cdot 2^2 + 0.01 \cdot 2^3 + \ldots + 0.01 \cdot 2^{28} + 0.01 \cdot 2^{29} \end{aligned}$$

As you can see most of the terms match, subtracting these simply leaves:

$$sum = -0.01 \cdot 2^0 + 0.01 \cdot 2^{30}$$

Which can be simplified to:

$$\begin{aligned} sum &= 0.01 \cdot 2^{30} - 0.01 \cdot 2^0 \\ &= 10{,}737{,}418.25 \end{aligned}$$

THE SOLUTION:

Option two is the better option for eleven months; however, if we redid our sums we'd see option one is better by nearly $5,000,000 in February.

GEOMETRIC SERIES

This leads to a general formula for the sum of a geometric series:

$$s = \frac{a(r^n - 1)}{(r - 1)}$$

where a is the first term, r is the common ratio (the multiplier between terms) and n is the number of terms.

Chapter

6

Money and Privacy

As we've strolled through the history of algebra we've found many situations in which algebra is put to good use, as well as a few light-hearted examples to boot. Now let's visit two areas in which algebra is most obvious in our everyday lives: money and privacy. We haven't the space to dissect the weirdness of modern finance or the labyrinthine encryptions of today's computers, so instead we'll visit the more accessible but equally fascinating subjects of interest and basic codes.

EXPONENTS LAWS

Before we get stuck into money, and interest rates in particular, we should have a quick recap of exponents. An exponent simply represents successive multiplications; that is to say, 2^5 (the ^{5} is the exponent) is the same as $2 \cdot 2 \cdot 2 \cdot 2 \cdot 2$.

A power has three parts, a coefficient, a base, and an exponent. For example, in $3x^5$, 3 is the coefficient, x is the base, and ^{5} is the exponent. Let's have a look at the laws governing exponents.

1) $x^n \cdot x^m = x^{n+m}$

When you multiply powers that have the same base, you simply add the exponents together. For example:

$$x^2 \cdot x^3 = x^5 \text{ or } (x \cdot x) \cdot (x \cdot x \cdot x) = (x \cdot x \cdot x \cdot x \cdot x)$$

2) $x^n \div x^m = x^{n-m}$

When you divide powers that have the same base you subtract their exponents. For example:

$$x^7 \div x^4 = x^3 \text{ or}$$

$$\frac{(x \cdot x \cdot x \cdot x \cdot x \cdot x \cdot x)}{(x \cdot x \cdot x \cdot x)} = \frac{(x \cdot x \cdot x \cdot \cancel{x \cdot x \cdot x \cdot x})}{(\cancel{x \cdot x \cdot x \cdot x})} = (x \cdot x \cdot x) = x^3$$

3) $(x^n)^m = x^{n \cdot m}$

When you raise a power to an exponent, multiply the exponents. For example:

$$(x^3)^2 = x^6 \text{ or}$$

$$(x^3) \cdot (x^3) = x^6 \text{ (using law 1)}$$

4) $(xy)^m = x^m y^m$

In other words, when you have two or more bases raised to the same exponent you can bring the exponent into each base. For example:

$$(xy)^3 = (xy)(xy)(xy) = (x \cdot x \cdot x)(y \cdot y \cdot y) = x^3 y^3$$

5) $\left(\frac{x}{y}\right)^m = \frac{x^m}{y^m}$

In other words, when you have a fraction raised to an exponent, the exponent can be brought into the numerator and the denominator. For example:

$$\left(\tfrac{x}{y}\right)^3 = \left(\tfrac{x}{y}\right)\left(\tfrac{x}{y}\right)\left(\tfrac{x}{y}\right) = \tfrac{(x \cdot x \cdot x)}{(y \cdot y \cdot y)} = \tfrac{x^3}{y^3}$$

6) $x^0 = 1$ where $x \neq 0$

An example by expansion:

$$\tfrac{x^3}{x^3} = \tfrac{(x \cdot x \cdot x)}{(x \cdot x \cdot x)} = \tfrac{(\cancel{x \cdot x \cdot x})}{(\cancel{x \cdot x \cdot x})} = 1$$

and by using law two $\frac{x^3}{x^3} = x^{3-3} = x^0$, since mathematics must maintain consistency then $x^0 = 1$, therefore anything to the zero power is one, except 0^0.

7) $x^{-m} = \frac{1}{x^m}$

This relates back to the law six and the reverse of law two, for example:

$$x^{-4} = \frac{1}{x^4} \text{ because}$$

$$x^{-4} = x^{0-4} = \frac{x^0}{x^4} = \frac{1}{x^4}$$

8) $\frac{1}{x^{-m}} = x^m$

Relates back to laws six and two, for example:

$$\frac{1}{x^{-4}} = x^4 \text{ because}$$

$$\frac{1}{x^{-4}} = \frac{x^0}{x^{-4}} = x^{0-(-4)} = x^{0+4} = x^4$$

Note that for laws seven and eight it's easier just to remember that you change the sign on the exponents when you change the side of the fraction; for example:

$$\frac{2^{-3}}{3^{-2}} = \frac{3^2}{2^3} = \frac{9}{8} = 1.125$$

You may notice that the introduction of these exponent laws follows the order of number sets introduced on pages 14–15. The first five exponent laws dealt with natural numbers; law six introduced a zero exponent thus introducing the whole number set; and laws seven and eight introduced the integer set to exponents. Now we will add two more laws—actually two parts of one law, but it's easier if we separate it into two—that will expand our laws to include rational numbers, or fractions.

9) $^n\sqrt{x} = x^{\frac{1}{n}}$

For example, lets find the square root of x. Firstly the square root should be written as $^2\sqrt{x}$ which would make it equal to $x^{\frac{1}{2}}$. The index on the square root is assumed but you see it on cube roots and up. So if we multiply the square root of x by itself we get:

$$\sqrt{x} \bullet \sqrt{x} = \sqrt{x \bullet x} = \sqrt{x^2} = x$$

If we multiplied the fractional exponent by itself we'd get the same result. (There are some restrictions, see box.) Therefore $^3\sqrt{x}$ would equal $x^{\frac{1}{3}}$ and so on. The last law is just an extension of law nine.

10) $^n\sqrt{x^m} = x^{\frac{m}{n}}$ or $(^n\sqrt{x})^m = x^{\frac{m}{n}}$

For example, $^3\sqrt{x^2} = x^{\frac{2}{3}}$ or $(^3\sqrt{x})^2 = x^{\frac{2}{3}}$

CAUTION REQUIRED

When dealing with exponents, we have to be careful because they can sometimes generate unusual results. For example, let's take the square root of minus two squared: $\sqrt{-2^2}$, following BEDMAS we square the –2 first to get 4, then the square root of 4 is 2. When you take $(\sqrt{(-2)})^2$, the square root is done first to give $\sqrt{2} \bullet i$, which we square to give $2 \bullet i^2$, which results in an answer of –2. As you can see the order has a big impact on the result.

Exercise 22 Two Problems with Interest

THE PROBLEM NO.1: PAYBACK WITH INTEREST

Allan needs some extra money to get his solo record project off the ground. He asks his friend Tony for a little cash. Allan says that if Tony could lend him \$450 that he will pay him back with interest in three years. They agree to a rate of five percent. Assuming simple interest, how much will Tony get?

THE METHOD:

First, although the question did say to assume simple interest, it's worth noting that we would have had to in any case because there was no mention of the compounding period (see pages 158–9).

The formula for calculating simple interest is refreshingly simple. It's $I = Prt$, where I is the interest gained, P is the principal (amount borrowed or invested depending on your point of view), r is the interest rate as a decimal, and t is the time in years. So in our problem we have:

$$I = Prt$$
$$I = (450)(0.05)(3)$$
$$I = 67.5$$

THE SOLUTION:

The interest is \$67.50 and the initial principal Tony lent Allan was \$450; therefore Tony will get \$517.50 back in three years.

THE PROBLEM NO.2: KING MIDAS IN REVERSE

Graham is convinced that his new song will be a big hit. He tells Bobby that if he lends him just \$780 today, he will pay him back in full (both the principal and some interest) in three years with ten crisp new \$100 bills—that's \$1000 to you and me. Assuming simple interest, what's the rate of return (the interest rate) that Bobby is getting?

THE METHOD:

Again we'll use the simple interest formula: $I = Prt$. This time we know P (the principal), which is 780; t (the time), which is three years; and I (the interest earned), which can be worked out as \$1000 – \$780, giving \$220. When plugged into the our formula this gives us the equation:

$$220 = (780)(r)(3)$$

One of the lovely things about multiplication is that the order in which it's performed is unimportant. This is called the "commutative law of multiplication," but it's really much simpler than it sounds. All it means is that 2 • 3 works out the same as 3 • 2.

Applied to our example, this means we can skip over the unknown r, and multiply the 3 by the 780 to get:

$$220 = 2340(r)$$

To get r alone we simply divide both sides by 2340:

$$\frac{220}{2340} = \frac{2340(r)}{2340} \text{ or } 0.094 = r$$

THE SOLUTION:

When we turn that decimal into a percentage (by multiplying it by 100) we find that Bobby gets a rate of return of 9.4%, in simple interest, over the three years.

EXPONENTIAL EQUATIONS

Exponents are used in finance (compound interest), biology (growth and decay), physics (radioactivity), chemistry (reaction rates), economics (supply and demand curves), and elsewhere. In my home province of British Columbia, the rate at which the pine forests are dying—due to the mountain pine beetle—is exponential.

An exponential equation is an equation in which the variable is in the exponent. This should not be confused with any equation with an exponent. So, for example, $2^x = 8$ is an exponential equation where $x^2 = 9$ is not.

However, before we take a look at a couple of real-world examples of exponential equations, let's get to grips with how to solve them.

Solving Exponential Equations

Solving exponential equations can sometimes be very straight forward. As an example, when seeing $2^x = 8$ many people will say $x = 3$, which is correct. This kind of intuitive feel for numbers is hard to explain, and the reality is that it's a very impressive calculation.

What happens is that you change the 8 into a power of 2 so that, $2^x = 2^3$ then, because the bases are the same you can compare the exponents and you find that $x = 3$.

Another example, $3^{2x-1} = 27$, can be solved the same way. Because 27 is equal to 3^3 we can write the equation as $3^{2x-1} = 27$. Now that the bases are the same we can compare the exponents and get $2x - 1 = 3$. To solve for x we add 1 to both sides so that we get $2x = 4$. Dividing both sides by 2 we finish with $x = 2$.

With this next example, $2 \cdot 3^x = 162$, there is the desire to multiply the 2 and 3 at the start. But wait a moment, only the 3 is "holding up" the x, not the 2. So the first step is to isolate the exponential 3^x by dividing both sides by 2, giving us $3^x = 81$. Then 81 is equal to 3^4 therefore $3^x = 3^4$ and finally $x = 4$.

This is all very nice, but some simple-looking equations like $2^x = 12$ cannot be solved in this manner. All we can do with this technique is say that the answer is between 3 and 4 ($2^3 = 8$ and $2^4 = 16$). To find a more exact solution requires logarithms (see pages 160–1).

The Mountain Pine Beetle

The mountain pine beetle is a little bug that's causing a big problem in British Columbia. Since the late 1990s, due to unseasonably warm winters, these little guys have been tearing though the forests of the interior of the province. The growth in the infested area is an exponential equation.

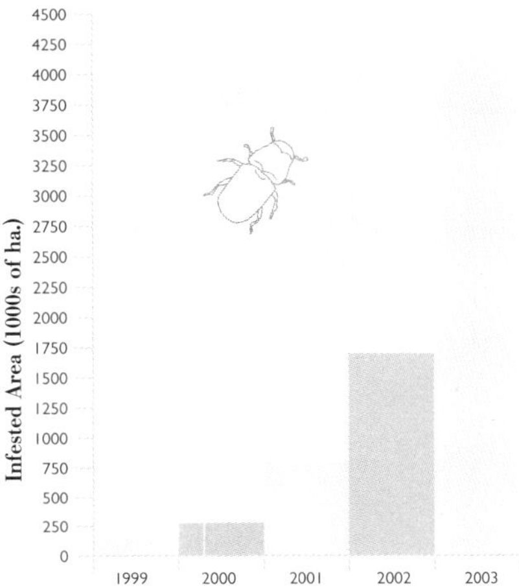

Year	Infested Area (1000s of ha.)	
1999	164.6	
2000	284.0	
2001	785.5	
2002	1968.6	*data from British Columbia*
2003	*4200.0*	*Ministry of Forests and Range*

Using a technique called regression, which we won't go into, an equation can be found that best matches the data in the table above—real life rarely works out perfectly.

The equation it gives is $A = 63(2.32)^t$, where A is the area infested and t is the number of years since 1998 (for 1999, $t = 1$); this allows foresters to predict the level of devastation. In practice the equation begins to fail as the food supply decreases. What happens is the pine beetles continue to spread until they run out of trees to munch on, when they die off.

Radioactive Decay

Another example of the importance of exponential equations can also be found in Canada. As it turns out Canada produces between half and two thirds of all medical isotopes (radioactive chemicals) in the world. In December 2007 a reactor producing the isotopes shut down, creating a global shortage. Many people complained that Chalk River Laboratories, where the isotopes are produced, should have created a stockpile. However, this exposes a common misunderstanding: When most people think about radioactivity, they think of long-term radioactivity because of "The Bomb." This is scary stuff, but many radioactive elements actually have short half-lives (the time it takes for half the matter to decay); for example, iodine-131, used in the treatment of thyroid cancer, has a half-life of just eight days.

So to stockpile iodine-131 the facility would have to compensate for radioactive decay by producing more than was needed to start with. For argument's sake, let's say that we needed 100 kg at the end of a shutdown lasting thirty-two days. The equation for a chemical's half-life is $F = I(\frac{1}{2})^{\frac{d}{8}}$, where F is the final amount, I is the initial amount, and d is the number of days. We know $F = 100$ and $d = 32$, so we can solve for I.

$$100 = I(\tfrac{1}{2})^{\frac{32}{8}}$$
$$100 = I(\tfrac{1}{2})^{4}$$
$$100 = I(\tfrac{1}{16})$$
$$1600 = I$$

Therefore Chalk River Laboratories would have to produce sixteen times the amount needed at the start of shutdown to have enough left at the end of the month.

Exercise 23 Compound Interest

THE PROBLEM:

Ralph has come into a bit of money: $2000 to be precise. He decides that he will put it in a Guaranteed Investment Certificate (GIC). He is going to invest it for fifteen years at six percent compounded annually. So, how much will he get back at the end of the fifteen years?

THE METHOD:

Compounding means that the interest made throughout the investment is added to the investment and interest is then gained on that interest. Because this investment is for fifteen years this process happens fifteen times. One approach to solving this is to calculate the interest after one year then add it to the principal. Then calculate the interest for the next year and add it to the principal. Then a table could be made like the one below:

This would continue until you reached the fifteenth year, but that's a lot of work! An easier approach is to use the formula $A = P(1+r)^n$, where A is the total amount you finish with, P is the principal (what you put in), r is the interest rate expressed as a decimal, and n is the number of years; therefore we get:

$$A = 2000(1 + 0.06)^{15}$$
$$A = 2000(1.06)^{15}$$
$$A = 2000(2.396558193)$$
$$A = 4793.11$$

Year	Principal	Interest ($I = Prt$)	New Principal
1	2000	120	2120
2	2120	127.2	2247.2
3	2247.2	134.832	2382.032
...	...	...	...

THE SOLUTION:

After fifteen years, Ralph will have \$4793.11 to spend. This demonstrates the power of compound interest, where your interest starts making more interest. If Ralph had been getting simple interest he would only have \$3800, which is almost a grand less.

Turn to pages 152–3 for more information on exponents.

DERIVING THE COMPOUND INTEREST FORMULA

The derivation of the compound interest formula follows the process opposite, where we use a table to calculate the money being earned.

If we look at the first year, the amount in the account will be the initial principal plus one year's interest or $P + I$. Now $I = Prt$, therefore we can rewrite this as $P + Prt$ (replacing I with the Prt). Since it's only one year ($t = 1$), we can write $P + Pr$. We can also write this as $1P + rP$. P is a common factor, therefore we can factor it out to get $P(1 + r)$. This represents the principal that starts year two.

So, in year two we again get the principal plus one year's interest, but for this year the principal is $P(1 + r)$ so this gives us $P(1 + r) + I$ where $I = P(1 + r)\bullet r$ (remember that $t = 1$). This gives a newer, more complicated, formula for the amount at the end of year two. It's $P(1 + r) + P(1 + r)\bullet r$.

Now $P(1 + r)$ is a common factor and can be factored out giving $P(1 + r)(1 + r)$ or $P(1 + r)^2$.

If this is hard to see, let's change the complicated bits into something easier, like a snowflake. Lets make $P(1 + r) =$ ❆. This will change $P(1 - r) + P(1 + r)\bullet r$ into ❆ + ❆r which we can write as 1❆ + r❆. We can factor out ❆ to get ❆$(1 + r)$. Now lets turn the ❆ back into $P(1 + r)$ to get $P(1 + r)(1 + r)$.

After three years we would have $P(1 + r)(1 + r)(1 + r)$ and at the end of four years $P(1 + r)(1 + r)(1 + r)(1 + r)$. From this you can see the pattern emerging, and as we've seen before, an exponent is simply successive multiplications, so this long string can be replaced by $A = P(1+r)^n$.

LOGARITHMS

Now we've met exponents it's time to meet their evil twin: logarithms. Mathematics is essentially about going somewhere and then getting back. Most of the time we learn about how to do something, then we learn how to reverse it. First we learn to add, then subtract. We learn to multiply, then divide. We learn about squares, then square roots. Exponents and logarithms are exactly the same, and a logarithm is simply the inverse of an exponent.

Logarithms: The New Kids in Town

Logarithms are a relatively new addition to mathematics. The first published account of logarithms was in 1614 by the Scottish mathematician John Napier (1550–1617), in his book *Mirifici Logarithmorum Canonis*. Around the same time, the Swiss mathematician, Joost Bürgi (1552–1632), discovered logarithms independently but did not publish his findings until four years after Napier.

Logarithms were initially developed to help with difficult multiplication and division problems, but since the advent of the calculator and computer this application has become pretty much redundant. Logarithms were the basis of the slide rule—a device carried around by every science and math geek in the '50s and '60s. However, by the '80s almost all of them had switched to the calculator—though they, myself among them, were still geeks!

However, logarithms still have uses today, mostly to help compare magnitudes of numbers. The most common logarithm uses a base of ten.

The function of a logarithm or "log" is to give the exponent on a base of ten that would equal a particular number. For example, log(10) is equal to 1. This is because $10 = 10^1$. The $\log(100) = 2$ because $100 = 10^2$. The $\log(1000) = 3$, the $\log(10000) = 4$, and so on. The $\log(250) \approx 2.4$ because $250 \approx 10^{2.4}$.

This has the effect of taking a wide range of numbers and reducing them to smaller, more-manageable numbers. In fact, all the numbers from one to a billion can be written as 0 to 9.

The Richter scale for earthquakes, the pH scale for acids and bases, and the dB (decibel) scale for sound intensity all use logarithms.

Practical Uses of Logarithms

One practical use of logarithms is the Richter Scale, which measures the magnitude of an earthquake. Because it's a logarithmic scale, a change of one on the Richter scale corresponds to a tenfold increase in magnitude. So, if one earthquake measures four while another measures seven, the difference in magnitude is not three but a thousand ($7 - 4 = 3$; $10^3 = 1000$). This is why an earthquake measuring four is hardly noticed while one measuring seven is very significant.

The pH scale measures how acidic or basic something is. It works in much the same way, but is the negative log of the hydrogen-ion concentration, therefore things that are more acidic have smaller numbers. The pH scale goes from 1 to 14, where 1 is the most acidic and 14 is the least acidic (most basic). As an example, let's say milk has a pH of 6.5 and soda has one of 2.5. This would make the soda 10,000 times more acidic ($6.5 - 2.5 = 4$; $10^4 = 10{,}000$) or conversely the milk 10,000 times more basic (generally speaking).

The decibel (dB) scale is very similar to the Richter scale with one added element to its calculation. For each ten points on the decibel scale there is a tenfold increase in sound intensity. The simplest way to work with the decibel scale is to divide the numbers by ten and treat it like the Richter scale.

For example, the difference between loud music at 100 dB and normal conversation at 60 dB is a difference in intensity of 10,000. To follow this calculation, divide both dB measures by ten, then subtract one from the other to find the difference, which is four. The difference in intensity is 10^4 or 10,000.

Hearing damage due to short-term exposure starts at 120 dB, and hearing damage due to long-term exposure (greater than eight hours) at 85 dB. For every 5 dB increase in intensity the exposure time decreases by half. Therefore, if you're being blasted with 90 dB you can last four hours before long-term damage. At 95 dB it's two hours, 100 dB is an hour, and so on. A level of 120 dB causes long-term damage after just four minutes.

• The decibel scale

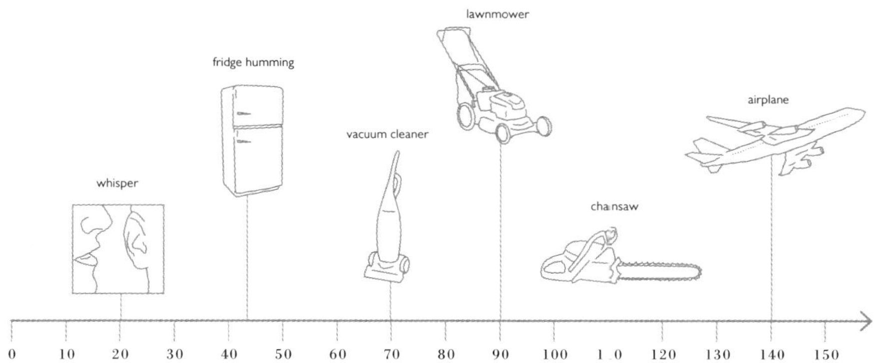

THE RULE OF 72

The "rule of 72" is a quick and easy way to estimate the time it takes for an investment to double in value given a particular interest rate. The formula is simply $time = \frac{72}{rate}$. As an example, the time it takes for an investment at six percent per annum to double is $\frac{72}{6}$ or twelve years. This is convenient because it only requires your brain and maybe a pencil and paper. It's a really useful rule of thumb, but it's not exact.

A Deeper Look

This rule is just an approximation of the exact solution. To get an exact answer for the above example we would need to solve the equation $2 = 1(1.06)^n$ for n. (This equation is the compound interest formula from page 158.) Here we invest a principal of \$1 and the amount given out is \$2. The variable n, for which we need to solve is in the exponent. This requires the use of logarithms from pages 160–1. The worked solution is shown below.

Compound interest formula:

$$A = P(1 + i)^n$$

Plug in an initial value (\$1) and final value (\$2) and 6% interest. Note: you can use any numbers but 1 and 2 are easiest: $2 = 1(1 + 0.06)^n$

Simplify the bracket: $2 = 1(1.06)^n$

Divide by one on both sides: $2 = 1.06^n$

log both sides: $\log(2) = \log(1.06)^n$

Move the n to the front (one of many properties of logarithms) so it becomes $\log(2) = n\log(1.06)$.

Divide by $\log(1.06)$: $\frac{\log(2)}{\log(1.06)} = n$ which gives:

$$11.9 = n$$

So twelve is pretty close and much easier; that's why the "rule of 72" is so good. There is a degree of error, though, and it's good to know it's there. In this case the approximate answer is twelve years, whereas the exact solution is eleven years 327 days or about one month sooner—but given that you're taking about 143 months compared to 144, I think that's no big deal.

Just How Accurate Is It?

The approximation and the exact solution do match at roughly 7.85%. The approximation is accurate to within a month for interest rates between

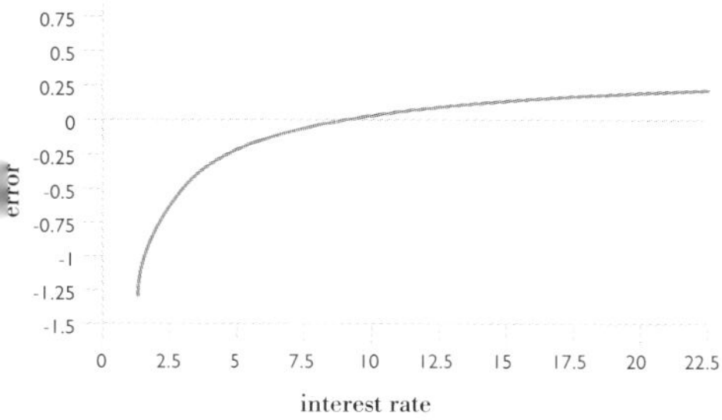

6.30% and 10.43%, accurate to within two months for rates between 5.26% and 15.66%. The rule overestimates the time required for interest rates less than 7.85%, so that means that when I am getting pathetically low returns from my investment I can at least be pleasantly surprised when my investment doubles quicker than the rule.

Two More Worked Examples

Determine the approximate time required for an investment to double if the rate is 8% per annum and 4% per annum. Then determine the exact time required at 8% and 4%.

An approximate solution:

At 8% $time = \frac{72}{8} = 9$ years

At 4% $time = \frac{72}{4} = 18$ years

An exact solution:

At 8%

$$\begin{aligned} 2 &= 1(1.08)^n \\ 2 &= 1.08^n \\ \log^2 &= \log 1.08^n \\ \log^2 &= n\log 1.08 \\ \frac{\log^2}{\log 1.08} &= n \\ 9.01 &= n \end{aligned}$$

At 4%

$$\begin{aligned} 2 &= 1(1.04)^n \\ 2 &= 1.04^n \\ \log^2 &= \log 1.04^n \\ \log^2 &= n\log 1.04 \\ \frac{\log^2}{\log 1.04} &= n \\ 17.67 &= n \end{aligned}$$

So, at 8% the "rule of 72" underestimates the time by two or three days. Over nine years, that's no big deal. At 4% the "rule of 72" overestimates the time needed by about 120 days or four months, so it's quite a lot less accurate but will at least give us a nice surprise. You may notice that the exact solution always reduces to log(2) divided by log(1 plus the rate).

Working in Reverse

I bought my first home back in spring 1998. As of spring 2008, my home was valued at twice what I paid for it ten years previously. At this point—before the housing meltdown, the stock market crash, the banking meltdown, the automotive slide, and all the other bad stuff going down—I was feeling pretty good about things and I wanted to know my rate of return. To do this I used the "rule of 72." This time I switched the variables, $rate = \frac{72}{time}$. This quick calculation told me I was getting a return on investment of 7.2%.

To be honest, I really don't want to know what my house is worth now.

Exercise 24

Freedom 65: Let's Hope

THE PROBLEM:

Roger and Pete are young mods who know all about their generation. Roger often claims he hopes to die before he gets old, but deep down he's thinking about his retirement. He plans to put $1000 away every birthday starting at twenty and stopping at twenty-nine. Pete wants to live a bit now and will start saving $1000 a year at thirty and stop at sixty-four. Assuming 6.6% interest per annum compounded yearly, when they both turn sixty-five who has the most saved?

THE METHOD:

First let's look at Roger. The investment he made at twenty is invested for forty-five years, the next investment for forty-four years, up to the last which is invested for thirty-six years. If we treat each individually we get the table below:

Now the column headed "Worth at 65" needs to be added together to determine his total retirement saving, therefore we get:

Savings $= 1000(1.066)^{36} + 1000(1.066)^{37} + \ldots + 1000(1.066)^{44} + 1000(1.066)^{45}$

Age Invested	Worth at 65	Age Invested	Worth at 65
20	$1000(1.066)^{45}$	25	$1000(1.066)^{40}$
21	$1000(1.066)^{44}$	26	$1000(1.066)^{39}$
22	$1000(1.066)^{43}$	27	$1000(1.066)^{38}$
23	$1000(1.066)^{42}$	28	$1000(1.066)^{37}$
24	$1000(1.066)^{41}$	29	$1000(1.066)^{36}$

This is a geometric series of ten terms with a first term a of $1000(1.066)^{36}$ and a common ratio r of 1.066. Using the formula for the sum of a geometric series:

$$S_n = \frac{a(r^n - 1)}{r - 1}$$

We can find the sum:

$$S_n = \frac{a(r^n - 1)}{r - 1}$$

$$S_n = \frac{1000(1.066)^{36}(1.066^{10} - 1)}{1.066 - 1}$$

By moving the exponents into the bracket (see pages 152–3) we get:

$$S_n = \frac{1000(1.066^{46} - 1.066^{36})}{0.066}$$

$$S_n = \$135{,}350.47$$

Now let's look at Pete. The investment made at age thirty is invested for thirty-five years, the next investment for thirty-four years, up to the last contribution at age sixty-four which is invested for one year. If we treat each one individually we get the table below (Note, there are terms missing):

$$\text{Savings} = 1000(1.066)^1 + 1000(1.066)^2 + \ldots + 1000(1.066)^{34} + 1000(1.066)^{35}$$

This is a geometric series of thirty-five terms with a first $1000(1.066)^1$ and a common ratio of 1.066. Using the formula for the sum of a geometric series: $s = \frac{a(r^n - 1)}{(r - 1)}$ we can find the sum:

$$S_n = \frac{1000(1.066)^1(1.066^{35} - 1)}{1.066 - 1}$$

We can move the $(1.066)^1$ into the other bracket to give:

$$S_n = \frac{1000(1.066^{36} - 1.066^1)}{0.066}$$

$$S_n = \$135{,}105.47$$

THE SOLUTION:

Although Roger only invested \$10,000 his accumulated amount was \$245 more than Pete's even though Pete contributed \$35,000.

It's a funny thing that retirement is the furthest from people's minds when it's actually the best time to invest. After all, time heals all wounds and corrects all stock market crashes—I hope.

Age Invested	Worth at 65	Age Invested	Worth at 65
30	$1000(1.066)^{35}$	62	$1000(1.066)^3$
31	$1000(1.066)^{34}$	63	$1000(1.066)^2$
32	$1000(1.066)^{33}$	64	$1000(1.066)^1$

Exercise 25

Freedom 55: You Need A Dream

THE PROBLEM:

Mike wants to retire at fifty-five. To do this he is going to set up a monthly deposit into his retirement account. The question is: How much should he put away each month?

THE METHOD:

There are a few details we need before we can begin the problem. First Mike's age: If he was fifty-four the question would be very different from if he was twenty—oh, to be twenty again!

Then there's his lifestyle. Anyone can retire at fifty-five, the question is whether it's a comfortable retirement. Presently Mike spends $2,250 per month. Retirement advisors suggest you should have 60% of your present income in retirement, due to reduced expenses. This would be $1,350 per month.

Third, is the length of his retirement. Many retirees worry about running out of cash if they live longer than they expect. If you think about it, this is a weird situation: they're presumably happy to live longer, but at the same time worried about it. Anyway, such existential ponderings to one side, Mike reckons he'll make it to eighty-five.

Fourth is the type of investments he gets. Mike invests a monthly amount at 6% per annum. This equates to a 0.5% per month $(\frac{6\%}{12})$. The term "compounded monthly" means that the interest starts earning interest each month.

Fifth is the rate of inflation. For this problem we will assume a constant rate of inflation at 2.5%.

Now that we have set the parameters of the problem, we can begin to work on a solution.

How Much Does He Need?

You might be thinking: "Hey we already said it would be $1,350," and in a sense that would be correct. However, that $1,350 is in today's dollars and we all know about increasing prices. In reality, Mike has to plan to have the equivalent of $1,350, rather than the exact figure. Given that he wants to be retired for thirty years, we will use a point fifteen years into retirement to do the equivalent dollar-value calculation. This means that he will have a better lifestyle (more purchasing power) at the beginning and a diminishing lifestyle (less purchasing power) toward the end. So, fifteen years into retirement Mike will be seventy, in other words fifty years from now. The formula for future equivalent dollars is just the compound interest formula using the inflation rate for the interest rate. That is to say the rate equals 0.025.

$$FD = PD(1 + rate)^{number\ of\ years}$$
$$FD = 1350(1 + 0.025)^{50}$$
$$FD = 1350(1.025)^{50}$$
$$FD = 4640$$

So what $1350 buys today you will need $4,640 to buy in fifty years.

Now we need to find out how much money Mike needs at fifty-five to create an annuity that pays the equivalent of $4,640 per month for thirty years. The formula is:

$$amount = payment\ \frac{(1 - (1 + rate)^{-\ number\ of\ periods})}{rate}$$

where *amount* is the unknown; *payment* is 4640; *rate* is 0.005 (0.5% as a decimal—remember we take the 6% and divide it by twelve months); *number of periods* is 360 (thirty years times twelve months). This gives:

$$amount = 4640\frac{(1 - (1 + 0.005)^{-360})}{0.005}$$

$$amount = 4640\frac{(1 - (1.005)^{-360})}{0.005}$$

$$amount = \$773,913.09$$

This is what Mike needs in order to retire comfortably when he's fifty-five.

How Much Should Mike Save?

Now we need to find out how much he needs to put away each month to acquire $773,913.09. To do this we apply the same formula as we did on page 165, but this time we'll just use the formula, we won't bother deriving it.

$$amount = payment\ (1 + rate)\frac{[(1 + rate)^{number\ of\ periods} - 1]}{rate}$$

where *amount* is $733,913.09; *payment* is our unknown; *rate* is 0.005 (again 6% divided by twelve months—as a decimal); *number of periods* is 420 (thirty-five years times twelve months).

$$733913.09 = payment(1+0.005)\frac{[(1.005)^{420} - 1]}{0.005}$$

$$733913.09 = payment(1.005)\frac{[(1.005)^{420} - 1]}{0.005}$$

$$\frac{733913.09}{(1431.83385)} = payment(1.005)$$

$512.57

THE SOLUTION:

So, if Mike wants the equivalent of $1,350 a month in retirement he needs to put $512.57 per month into a retirement account. This is in today's dollars, so obviously there's the potential for variation. This is one of the big problems with self-directed and defined contribution plans—you have to be vigilant.

CODES AND CIPHERS

Moving on from money, we reach the related field of privacy. After all, where would we be without password-protected accounts, personal identification numbers, and the like? The ability to send and receive messages without them being read is very important; and the art and mathematics of cryptography, which includes codes and ciphers, has been around since the time of the ancient Greeks.

Throughout most of history, only the most secret of political, military, or economic secrets were sent in code or cipher, and only a select few were involved with cryptography. However, in the modern age almost everyone in the developed world deals with cryptography in our daily lives. Every time you use your credit or debit card, every time you use a "secure" website, every time you unlock your car remotely, you're using cryptography. Yet many people remain unaware of its significance.

Codes

Codes and ciphers are actually different things, though many people use the words interchangeably. Strictly speaking, a code is a secret language in which a word is given meanings in place of its normal ones.

This is the kind of thing that you hear in classic spy movies, and that was broadcast to the French Resistance during the Second World War in the form of such oblique messages as "Les carottes sont cuites" ("The carrots are cooked"). The American forces also employed code talkers, most famously Navajos, who adapted their language to send secret military messages.

Ciphers

Unlike codes, ciphers are not a secret language, but rather a way to change language so it's unintelligible to those without a key. A key is a system to encipher and decipher messages. A sender will encipher "plain text" to create a "ciphered text"; while the receiver will use the same key to decipher the "ciphered text" back into "plain text."

The trick to a good encryption is the amount of work that is required for an interloper to find or crack the key. The longer it takes, the better the cipher.

Solving Ciphers

To conclude our journey through algebra we'll take a closer look at two enjoyable ciphers: the simple Caesar cipher (see pages 170–1) and the slightly more complex Vigenère cipher (see pages 172–3), which is an advancement on the Caesar cipher, and was still in use during the American Civil War.

Both of these are substitution ciphers, in which letters are substituted for one another. It's a form of ciphering that you may already be familiar with from the cryptograms that appear in Sunday newspapers.

These puzzles can be challenging, but their solution only requires the application of an algorithm and a degree of patience. A good first step to cracking such ciphers is to make a what is called a letter-frequency chart; after all, e, t, and a account for almost a third of letters used in written English. Knowing this gives you an idea which ciphered letters are really e, t, or a, as well as others. You also have other clues; for example, a one-letter word will be "I" or "a"—assuming the spacing is maintained. The most common two-letter words are "of," "to," "in," and "it"; and the most common three-letter words are "the," "and," "for," and "are."

Some ciphers don't require "encipherment" as such, but are hidden within reams of unimportant text. In these ciphers, often only one letter out of ten or twenty is meaningful and the rest are garbage. Finding the ones with meaning is like panning for gold: you sift through a lot of dirt to find your nugget.

A stencil cipher is one example of this form. The message sender writes a long and misleading text, then the receiver covers it with a sheet that has holes in it. This covers the unimportant text, but leaves the important letters and the message exposed. However, stencil ciphers can be broken over time, and it's also possible to see messages that may not be intended.

Cracking the Enigma

Perhaps the most famous examples of ciphers are those generated by the German Enigma machine during the Second World War. The machine used rotors to generate complex ciphers for the encryption and decryption of secret messages. However, Allied decryption efforts at Bletchley Park, England—aided by captured Enigma machines—were successful, and are credited with hastening the war's end.

• German signal troops communicate during the Second World War using what is described as a "teletype," but which actually resembles the Enigma encryption machine.

Exercise 26

Caesar Ciphers

THE PROBLEM:

Melanie and Victoria want to plan a surprise party for Emma. They spend all their time chatting online, so Melanie and Victoria need a code that even if Emma sees it she will not understand. Use the Caesar cipher to encode the message: "THE PARTY FOR EMMA WILL BE ON NOVEMBER NINTH"; and decode the reply: "QRYHPEHU QLQWK VRXQGV JRRG VHH BRX WKHUH."

THE METHOD:

Now, the Caesar cipher isn't very secure, so I wouldn't recommend it to any budding secret agents. However, it's nice and simple, so it's great for the relatively unimportant kind of message that the girls want to send.

First, Melanie and Victoria need to decide their "letter shift," which can be any number from one to twenty-six. Then they write out the alphabet along a line. Beneath this they write out a second alphabet, but this time they apply their chosen letter shift. For example, the letter A is the first letter of the alphabet, so a letter shift of three means that they should write D, the fourth letter of the alphabet, underneath it. From there they can go on to write out the full alphabet, matching each letter in the top line to one with the letter shift applied in the bottom line.

Next they move to the letter they want in the top row, and then replace it with the matching letter in the bottom row. For the first few letters of their message, "T" becomes "W"; "H" becomes "K"; "E" becomes "H"; and so on. The code isn't particularly sophisticated, so we'll just

A	B	C	D	E	F	G	H	I	J	K	L	M	N	O	P	Q	R	S	T	U	V	W	X	Y	Z
D	E	F	G	H	I	J	K	L	M	N	O	P	Q	R	S	T	U	V	W	X	Y	Z	A	B	C

leave spaces where they occur in the original message. Our encoded message becomes "WKH SDUWB IRU HPPD ZLOO EH RQ QRYHPEHU QLQWK."

To decode the reply of "QRYHPEHU QLQWK VRXQGV JRRG VHH BRX WKHUH" we work from the bottom alphabet up to the top alphabet, therefore a "Q" becomes an "N," an "R" becomes an "O," and so on. Our decoded message becomes "November ninth sounds good see you there."

The Caesar cipher can also be shown as a formula. But first we need to assign a number to each letter, so A = 0, B = 1, and so on. To encrypt we use the formula $E_n(x) = (x + n)\ (mod\ 26)$ where x is the letter and n is the value of the letter shift. All that "*mod* 26" means is that whenever you go past the twenty-sixth letter of the alphabet you simply loop back to the start. So, for the first letter of our example, T is the twentieth letter in the alphabet, and the letter shift is three. So $E_n(x) = (20 + 3)$ or $E_n(x) = 23$. This means we replace T with the twenty-third letter of the alphabet, which is W.

As you may have guessed, decryption uses the formula: $D_n(x) = (x - n)\ (mod\ 26)$. To reverse the example we've just given, simply plug in $D_n(x) = (23 - 3)$ so $D_n(x) = 20$. This means we replace W with the twentieth letter of the alphabet, which is T.

THE SOLUTION:

The encoded message "THE PARTY FOR EMMA WILL BE ON NOVEMBER NINTH," becomes "WKH SDUWB IRU HPPD ZLOO EH RQ QRYHPEHU QLQWK." The decoded message of "QRYHPEHU QLQWK VRXQGV JRRG VHH BRX WKHUH," becomes "NOVEMBER NINTH SOUNDS GOOD SEE YOU THERE."

DYH FDHVDU

A Caesar cipher can use a shift of any amount, but it's said that Caesar used a shift of three like the above exercise. However, with only twenty-six options (for the English alphabet) the Caesar cipher is easy to crack. It probably worked well for Caesar because so few people were literate.

A more modern use is "rotate by thirteen," or ROT13, a Caesar cipher that is commonly used online to conceal things like the punchlines to jokes from a casual glance.

• **Julius Caesar was supposedly the first to use the cipher that bears his name.**

Exercise 27

Vigenère Ciphers

THE PROBLEM:

Melanie and Victoria soon realize that their cipher is relatively easy to crack so they decide to implement the stronger Vigenère cipher. Instead of a letter shift, they choose a keyword. Use the Vigenère cipher to encode "OUR COVER IS BLOWN, WE NEED TO MAKE NEW PLANS" and decode "OIKSGW, HJBG PXK EBDJXF KL AWVV DXHVXF UXQWKWVR WU TGUNFGW"

THE METHOD:

Melanie and Victoria decide their keyword will be a three-letter abbreviation of the month in which the message is sent: Jan, Feb, Mar, and so on.

BLAISE DE VIGENÈRE

Blaise de Vigenère was a French diplomat who lived from 1523 to 1596. He was the developer of a cipher system, but rather oddly not the one which bears his name. The Vigenère cipher was actually described by Giovan Bellaso in 1553.

Melanie encodes the following message for Victoria, sent in September: "OUR COVER IS BLOWN, WE NEED TO MAKE NEW PLANS."

First she needs a "tabula recta" to help her encode the message. (The Vigenère cipher is just a Caesar cipher where the letter shift is not constant.) For example, in the previous exercise we shifted all letters by three; this relates to row D in the tabula recta opposite. With the Vigenère cipher we change the shift by using a keyword, so the cipher changes for each letter.

Melanie and Victoria are using a rotating keyword, in other words one that changes monthly. So for Melanie's message the keyword is "SEP." This

	A	B	C	D	E	F	G	H	I	J	K	L	M	N	O	P	Q	R	S	T	U	V	W	X	Y	Z
A	A	B	C	D	E	F	G	H	I	J	K	L	M	N	O	P	Q	R	S	T	U	V	W	X	Y	Z
B	B	C	D	E	F	G	H	I	J	K	L	M	N	O	P	Q	R	S	T	U	V	W	X	Y	Z	A
C	C	D	E	F	G	H	I	J	K	L	M	N	O	P	Q	R	S	T	U	V	W	X	Y	Z	A	B
D	D	E	F	G	H	I	J	K	L	M	N	O	P	Q	R	S	T	U	V	W	X	Y	Z	A	B	C
E	E	F	G	H	I	J	K	L	M	N	O	P	Q	R	S	T	U	V	W	X	Y	Z	A	B	C	D
F	F	G	H	I	J	K	L	M	N	O	P	Q	R	S	T	U	V	W	X	Y	Z	A	B	C	D	E
G	G	H	I	J	K	L	M	N	O	P	Q	R	S	T	U	V	W	X	Y	Z	A	B	C	D	E	F
H	H	I	J	K	L	M	N	O	P	Q	R	S	T	U	V	W	X	Y	Z	A	B	C	D	E	F	G
I	I	J	K	L	M	N	O	P	Q	R	S	T	U	V	W	X	Y	Z	A	B	C	D	E	F	G	H
J	J	K	L	M	N	O	P	Q	R	S	T	U	V	W	X	Y	Z	A	B	C	D	E	F	G	H	I
K	K	L	M	N	O	P	Q	R	S	T	U	V	W	X	Y	Z	A	B	C	D	E	F	G	H	I	J
L	L	M	N	O	P	Q	R	S	T	U	V	W	X	Y	Z	A	B	C	D	E	F	G	H	I	J	K
M	M	N	O	P	Q	R	S	T	U	V	W	X	Y	Z	A	B	C	D	E	F	G	H	I	J	K	L
N	N	O	P	Q	R	S	T	U	V	W	X	Y	Z	A	B	C	D	E	F	G	H	I	J	K	L	M
O	O	P	Q	R	S	T	U	V	W	X	Y	Z	A	B	C	D	E	F	G	H	I	J	K	L	M	N
P	P	Q	R	S	T	U	V	W	X	Y	Z	A	B	C	D	E	F	G	H	I	J	K	L	M	N	O
Q	Q	R	S	T	U	V	W	X	Y	Z	A	B	C	D	E	F	G	H	I	J	K	L	M	N	O	P
R	R	S	T	U	V	W	X	Y	Z	A	B	C	D	E	F	G	H	I	J	K	L	M	N	O	P	Q
S	S	T	U	V	W	X	Y	Z	A	B	C	D	E	F	G	H	I	J	K	L	M	N	O	P	Q	R
T	T	U	V	W	X	Y	Z	A	B	C	D	E	F	G	H	I	J	K	L	M	N	O	P	Q	R	S
U	U	V	W	X	Y	Z	A	B	C	D	E	F	G	H	I	J	K	L	M	N	O	P	Q	R	S	T
V	V	W	X	Y	Z	A	B	C	D	E	F	G	H	I	J	K	L	M	N	O	P	Q	R	S	T	U
W	W	X	Y	Z	A	B	C	D	E	F	G	H	I	J	K	L	M	N	O	P	Q	R	S	T	U	V
X	X	Y	Z	A	B	C	D	E	F	G	H	I	J	K	L	M	N	O	P	Q	R	S	T	U	V	W
Y	Y	Z	A	B	C	D	E	F	G	H	I	J	K	L	M	N	O	P	Q	R	S	T	U	V	W	X
Z	Z	A	B	C	D	E	F	G	H	I	J	K	L	M	N	O	P	Q	R	S	T	U	V	W	X	Y

means that we use rows "S," "E," and "P" of the table above.

	A	B	C	D	E	F	G	H	I	J	K	L	M	N	O	P	Q	R	S	T	U	V	W	X	Y	Z
S	S	T	U	V	W	X	Y	Z	A	B	C	D	E	F	G	H	I	J	K	L	M	N	O	P	Q	R
E	E	F	G	H	I	J	K	L	M	N	O	P	Q	R	S	T	U	V	W	X	Y	Z	A	B	C	D
P	P	Q	R	S	T	U	V	W	X	Y	Z	A	B	C	D	E	F	G	H	I	J	K	L	M	N	O

To encode the message the first letter in the message uses row "S", the second uses row "E," and the third uses row "P." The number of letters in the keyword (the "period" of the cipher key) is three, so the fourth letter goes back to row "S" again, and the loop continues.

This means "OUR COVER IS BLOWN, WE NEED TO MAKE NEW PLANS," becomes "GYG USKWV XK FAGAC, OI CWIS LS BSOT FIL HPPFW."

To decode the reply from Victoria "OIKSGW, HJBG PXK EBDJXF KL AWVV DXHVXF UXQWKWVR WU TGUNFGW" Melanie uses rows "O," "C," and "T" of the tabula recta because the message was sent in October.

	A	B	C	D	E	F	G	H	I	J	K	L	M	N	O	P	Q	R	S	T	U	V	W	X	Y	Z
O	O	P	Q	R	S	T	U	V	W	X	Y	Z	A	B	C	D	E	F	G	H	I	J	K	L	M	N
C	C	D	E	F	G	H	I	J	K	L	M	N	O	P	Q	R	S	T	U	V	W	X	Y	Z	A	B
T	T	U	V	W	X	Y	Z	A	B	C	D	E	F	G	H	I	J	K	L	M	N	O	P	Q	R	S

To decode, she finds an "O" in row "O" and sees that it lines up with an "A"; then she finds an "I" in row "C"and sees it lines up with a "G." Next she finds a "K" in row "T" which lines up with "R." She continues to cycle through the rows until she has deciphered the message.

The enciphered reply from Victoria of "OIKSGW, HJBG PXK EBDJXF KL AWVV DXHVXF UXQWKWVR WU TGUNFGW" becomes "AGREED, THIS NEW CIPHER IS MUCH BETTER. SECURITY IS ASSURED."

THE SOLUTION:

The plain text message of "OUR COVER IS BLOWN, WE NEED TO MAKE NEW PLANS" becomes "GYG USKWV XK FAGAC, OI CWIS LS BSOT FIL HPPFW" when enciphered.

While the enciphered reply of "OIKSGW, HJBG PXK EBDJXF KL AWVV DXHVXF UXQWK WVR WU TGUNFGW" becomes "AGREED, THIS NEW CIPHER IS MUCH BETTER. SECURITY IS ASSURED" when deciphered into plain text.

INDEX

TERMS AND SYMBOLS

Terms and symbols are explained where they are introduced within the text; however, a few are noted here for the sake of clarity.

Base the number or variable that forms part of a power and is acted upon by an exponent; for example, in the term x^2 the x is the base.

Coefficient a constant value that multiplies a variable; for example, in the term $3x^2$ the 3 is the coefficient.

Equation an equation always includes an equals sign; for example, $3x - 5 = 13$. Note, $\approx$ denotes "approximately equal to."

Exponent the number or variable that forms part of a power and indicates the repeated multiplication of the base by itself; for example, in x^2 the ^{2} is the exponent, and is equivalent to $x \cdot x$, while x^3 is equivalent to $x \cdot x \cdot x$; note that x implies x^1.

Expression a collection of numbers and variables that has neither an equals nor an inequality sign; for example, $(3x - 4) + 5$.

Inequation an inequation has an inequality sign where the equals sign would normally be; for example, $3(x + 2) \leq 2x + 5$. Inequality signs include: $\neq$ (not equal to); $<$ (less than); $>$ (greater than); $\geq$ (greater than or equal to); and $\leq$ (less than or equal to).

Like terms terms with the same type and number of variables; for example, $6x^2$ and $8x^2$ are like terms, but $6x^2$ and $8x$ are not because the exponents are different, and neither are $6y^2$ and $8x^2$ because the variables differ.

Multiplication the symbol • is used in place of "x" to avoid confusion with the variable x. Multiplication is also indicated by closed-up numerals or variables. For example, both $x \cdot y$ or xy can be read as "x multiplied by y."

Operation a mathematical action; for example, addition or subtraction.

Plus-Minus indicated by the symbol $\pm$, within the context of algebra this represents two equations within one formula, and implies two solutions. For example, the formula $(x + 3) = \pm 7$ leads to two correct solutions $x = -10$ and $x = 4$.

Polynomial a collection of terms that include whole-number exponents. A polynomial of one term is a monomial; one with two terms is a binomial; and one with three terms is a trinomial.

Power strictly speaking, the combination of base and exponent; however, in everyday language it is often used to refer solely to the exponent.

Term a number or variable, or the product of several numbers or variables, that is separated from another term by addition or subtraction.

Variable a symbol, often x or y, used to represent a variable value in a term.